A Populist, a Pope,
and the Soul of a Nation

A Populist, a Pope,
and the Soul of a Nation

Fratelli Tutti in an Age of Global Trumpism

JACQUELINE MURRAY BRUX

RESOURCE *Publications* · Eugene, Oregon

A POPULIST, A POPE, AND THE SOUL OF A NATION
Fratelli Tutti in an Age of Global Trumpism

Resource Publications
An Imprint of Wipf and Stock Publishers
199 W. 8th Ave., Suite 3
Eugene, OR 97401

www.wipfandstock.com

PAPERBACK ISBN: 978-1-6667-7841-0
HARDCOVER ISBN: 978-1-6667-7842-7
EBOOK ISBN: 978-1-6667-7843-4

VERSION NUMBER 050823

Thomas R. Smith, "Dear Future," *International Times,* https://internationaltimes.it/dear-future, 1–28–2023.

Thomas R. Smith, "Hand in Pocket, i.m. George Floyd," *Storm Island,* Red Dragonfly Press, 5–30–2020.

I dedicate this book to the women of the world—to those who do the back-breaking labor; to those who suffer from poverty, deprivation, and hardship; to those who are hurt by violence and pain; and especially to those who have lost their children.
May God cradle you in her arms and bring you comfort.

Contents

KNOWING THE EXPLOITED

WHERE DO WE GO FROM HERE?

Preface

THIS BOOK IS BASED on the words of Pope Francis in his encyclical, *Fratelli Tutti* (Brothers and Sisters All),[1] former president Donald Trump (mostly during his 2016 candidacy and four years as president), and President Joe Biden (during his presidency). We see the words of many others who have spoken in their midst and since then as well.

Unless otherwise indicated, U.S. data are from the U.S. Census Bureau, www.census.gov; and international data are from the World Bank, *World Development Indicators*, www.wdi.worldbank/tables.[2] Unless otherwise noted, cited newspaper articles are originally published or reprinted in the *Minneapolis Star Tribune*.

1. Pope Francis, *Fratelli Tutti*, the Vatican, October 3, 2020.

2. Many people across the country and across the globe refer to the United States as "America" and to U.S. residents as "Americans." Technically, the "Americas" include all of North America (the United States, Canada, and Mexico), Central America, South America, and the Caribbean Islands. Nevertheless, since the term "America" is so widely used in reference to the United States, we will do so as well.

Acknowledgements

THANK YOU FOR EVERYTHING, *Keith*.

Capitalized Words

I'VE CAPITALIZED THESE WORDS throughout the book.

AIDS   Acquired Immune Deficiency Syndrome

ANTIFA   anti-fascist

CNN   Cable News Network.

COVID-19   Coronavirus Disease 2019

DACA   Deferred Action on Childhood Arrivals

ESPN   Entertainment and Sports Programming Network

ICE   Immigration and Customs Enforcement

LGBTQ   lesbian, gay, bisexual, transgender, and queer (or questioning).

MSNBC   Microsoft National Broadcasting Company

NATO   North Atlantic Treaty Organization

TPS   Temporary Protected Status

UN   United Nations

Introduction

For Whom Do We Care?

THIS BOOK IS NOT solely about Donald Trump. It is not just about multiple populist politicians that include the United Kingdom's former Prime Minister Boris Johnson, Hungary's Prime Minister Viktor Orbán, Brazil's former President Jair Bolsonaro, and India's Prime Minister Narendra Modi, though these and other populists are discussed.

Nor is the book about Pope Francis, though he features prominently; nor is it about President Biden. Most importantly, the book doesn't address populism alone, though this and related rightwing ideologies are carefully examined. No, this book is about people—many, many people. They include people of color and victims of bigotry. They comprise prisoners facing capital punishment and families facing eviction. They include people discarded amid violence and forgotten in poverty. They include Muslims, the people intuitively emphasized by the pope, especially the Rohingya, Uighurs, and Yazidis, as well as the people of Palestine, Yemen, Syria, and Somalia. They include Africans in Tigray, Eurasians in Nagorno-Karabakh, Afghans in French homeless camps, and Mexicans in the hidden corners of America. They are comprised of desperate immigrants washed up on the shores of the Mediterranean and asylum-seekers drowned in the Rio Grande. They include Iraqi children killed by unexploded cluster bombs and Syrian families killed by deliberately detonated ones. They are represented by Black Lives Matter in Minneapolis, São Paulo, and Cape Town. They include America's elderly left vulnerable as a nation tires of coronavirus precautions, and South Africa's poor "volunteers" used to test a new vaccine. They contain the trafficked and the addicted; the cotton suicides and missing Indigenous women; and the child, slave, and sweatshop laborers. They include so many more.

These are the people for whom Pope Francis calls us to love as sisters and brothers. They are the ones manipulated, scapegoated, denigrated, and discarded by populism. They are the people exploited by unrestrained capitalism. We may know *of* them, but we may not *know* them. As we come to know their stories, we come to see them as people; and when we see them as people, they become our sisters and brothers. Only then can we truly care.

The pope's message is addressed to all people—those of any faith and those of no faith. He wants us to become better people, to take care of each other. President Joe Biden's pursuit is similar, as he battles to make ours a better country—a battle he fights for "the soul of the nation." Thus, we have a spiritual leader, a religious president, and a disgraced, twice impeached, indicted, and arrested former president who controls his party and threatens retribution for those who are disloyal. He appeals to white Christian nationalists though he himself is not religious. Where does this leave us? Where do we go from here?

QUESTION(S) FOR DISCUSSION

1. Who are the "discarded" and "exploited?" Explain.

2. Do you agree that President Biden is religious?

3. Do you agree that former President Trump is not religious?

The Story of a Visit

Chapter 1

With Whom Do We Visit?

THE STORY OF A VISIT

POPE FRANCIS TELLS A story about Saint Francis of Assisi. The story is ordinary enough to appeal to us in the simplicity of one man visiting another man—the story of Saint Francis visiting the Muslim Sultan Malik-El-Kamil in Egypt in the early 1200's. Indeed, it reminds many of us of a similar story of one woman visiting another woman—Mary visiting her cousin Elizabeth amid their pregnancies (Lk 1:39-45). These are everyday visits of "sisters and brothers" in familial friendship. Yet like the visit of Mary and Elizabeth, the visit of Saint Francis and the Sultan was a stunning event with profound revelations.

> [Saint] Francis went to meet the Sultan . . . [and] understood that 'God is love and those who abide in love abide in God' (1 Jn 4:16).[1]

With these words, Pope Francis relayed the significance of:

> one who approaches others, not to draw them into his own life, but to help them become ever more fully themselves.[2]

To help them become ever more fully themselves. Who among us would pause to realize we are called to help Muslims become better Muslims? Or Jews become better Jews? Or even Christians become better Christians?

---

1. Pope Francis, *Fratelli Tutti*, 3. Numbers refer to paragraphs in *Fratelli Tutti*.
2. Pope Francis, *Fratelli Tutti*, 4.

The visit between Saint Francis and the Sultan took place during the Crusades, a time Pope Francis says was, "bristling with watchtowers and defensive walls."[3] It was not unlike our own time, brimming with border walls and barbed-wire fencing. Refugees fleeing violence are offered no safety. People escaping the ravages of climate change are refused a safe harbor. And families facing abysmal poverty and brutal conditions of hardship and deprivation are provided no refuge. Instead, and sadly, people are held in contempt for their poverty and their flight. They are disparaged for their religion, race, and nationality and are often pummeled with racist, Islamophobic, and xenophobic tropes and stereotypes. Indeed, hate speech is perpetrated by leaders and politicians who wish to arouse fear among their supporters and division among the people.

Saint Francis refused to disparage the Islamic Sultan. Instead, he sought to make him a better Muslim.

A MODERN-DAY VISIT

Pope Francis himself made a visit not unlike the visit of Saint Francis. In early 2019, the pope visited the Grand Imam Ahmad Al-Tayyab in Abu Dhabi, where together they declared:

> God has created all human beings equal in rights, duties and dignity, and has called them to live together as brothers and sisters.[4]

The pope added,

> It is my desire that, in this our time, by acknowledging the dignity of each human person, we can contribute to the rebirth of a universal aspiration to fraternity. Fraternity between all men and women.[5]

Fraternity—men and women. Fratelli—brothers and sisters. Fratelli Tutti—brothers and sisters *all*. No one is discarded, no one is exploited, and no one is marginalized.

In 2019, then candidate Joe Biden launched his campaign for the presidency with a video in which he stated, "We are in the battle for the soul

---

3. Pope Francis, *Fratelli Tutti*, 4.

4. Pope Francis, *Fratelli Tutti*, 5.

5. Pope Francis, *Fratelli Tutti*, 8.

of this nation."[6] The video showed images of white supremacists marching in Charlottesville, Virginia, among a group of their supporters that Donald Trump insisted included many fine people. It wasn't until after Biden won the election and became president-elect, he confidently declared that "in this battle for the soul of America, democracy prevailed."[7]

Perhaps democracy did prevail, but its assurance was short-lived. On January 6, 2021, a mob that included white supremacists, neo-Nazi's, and white Christian nationalists invaded the nation's Capital Building, leaving five people dead within a day of the riot. About 140 members of law enforcement were injured as rioters attacked them with flagpoles, baseball bats, stun guns, bear spray, and pepper spray. Four other officers who responded to the attack killed themselves within seven months. The insurgents sought House Speaker Nancy Pelosi by name and brought with them a noose and gallows for the purpose of hanging Vice President Mike Pence.

Clearly, the battle for our country's soul wasn't over, perhaps suggesting it is a never-ending one. Once again, on September 1, 2022, President Biden felt compelled to speak of "the soul of the nation." He declared that "Donald Trump and the MAGA Republicans represent an extremism that threatens the very foundations of our republic."[8] He was right. As it turns out, the white supremacy of a former president had infected and revealed an evil so endemic in his party that it threatens our nation's very soul. And once again, we must ask: where does this leave us? With an authoritarian populist dictating the terms of an entire political party? With a president bent on saving the nation's soul? With a pope who is cherished yet misunderstood as he mourns those discarded by populist ideology and exploited by capitalist dogma?

And once again, we must also ask, you and me: where do we go from here? Do we celebrate our "differences of origin, nationality, color, [and] religion"?[9] Do we help others "become ever more fully themselves"?[10] Do we seek the soul of a nation? If not, are we not complicit in any evil around us?

And finally, with whom do we visit? Like St. Francis, do we walk "alongside the poor, the abandoned, the infirm and the outcast, the least

6. Jones, "Biden Launches."

7. Herman, "Democracy Prevailed."

8. Camera, "Trump Extremism."

9. Pope Francis, *Fratelli Tutti*, 3.

10. Pope Francis, *Fratelli Tutti*, 3.

of his [our] brothers and sisters"?[11] These visits are indeed compassionate encounters that bring healing. They are extolled by Pope Francis as the
familial love in which he asks us to partake.

> Let us dream, then, as a single human family, as fellow travelers
> sharing the same flesh, as children of the same earth which is our
> common home, each of us bringing the richness of his or her be-
> liefs and convictions, each of us with his or her own voice, broth-
> ers and sisters all.[12]

Let's do this—you and me. Let's seek to understand the pope's words.
Let's learn about the discarded and exploited. Let's bring about the healing
our visits can call forth. Let's do this together. Let's do this as sisters and
brothers.

QUESTIONS FOR DISCUSSION

1. What is the meaning of "*Fratelli Tutti*"?

2. The concept of "visits" is used as a metaphor. What do you think it
means?

3. With whom do we visit?

11. Pope Francis, *Fratelli Tutti*, 2.
12. Pope Francis, *Fratelli Tutti*, 8.

Understanding The Ideologies

Chapter 2

Populism and Other Rightwing Ideologies
An Overview

POPE FRANCIS WRITES LONGINGLY of a forgotten era of global integration when nations moved away from war and found ways to come together.

> For decades, it seemed that the world had learned a lesson from its many wars and disasters and was slowly moving towards various forms of integration . . . In some countries and regions, attempts at reconciliation and rapprochement proved fruitful, while others showed great promise.[1]

Sadly, many countries today are moving in the opposite direction. In the pope's words, they are embracing ideologies of "selfishness"—going it alone in the search for their "national interest." Pope Francis states that:

> a concept of popular and national unity influenced by various ideologies is creating new forms of selfishness and a loss of the social sense under the guise of defending national interests.[2]

With the words "popular" and "national," the pope is referencing the "ideologies" of populism and nationalism. He notes that these two rightwing ideologies can ultimately be associated with authoritarianism, described by Pope Francis as a breach of our very foundations and conventions.

---

1. Pope Francis, *Fratelli Tutti,* 10.
2. Pope Francis, *Fratelli Tutti,* 11.

This becomes all the more serious when, whether in cruder or more subtle forms, it leads to the usurpation of institutions and laws.[3]

Finally, the pope addresses both populism and capitalism (which he refers to as liberalism).

Lack of concern for the vulnerable can hide behind a populism that exploits them demagogically for its own purposes, or a liberalism that serves the economic interests of the powerful. In both cases, it becomes difficult to envisage an open world that makes room for everyone, including the most vulnerable, and shows respect for different cultures.[4]

Thus, the opposition of Pope Francis to the ideologies of populism and unrestrained capitalism rests on the harm they inflict on vulnerable people. To use the pope's terminology, we will see how populism "discards" people and capitalism "exploits" them. These then are the "marginalized people" frequently referenced by the pope. We will consider their stories in future chapters.

Populism and nationalism are ideologies, as are authoritarianism and capitalism. Authoritarianism is also a political system (as is its opposite, democracy), and capitalism is additionally an economic system (as is its counterpart, socialism). First and foremost, we address populism.

POPULISM

Populism can take multiple forms in different times and places. It nevertheless encompasses certain characteristics that are typical across different times and locales.

Populism is an ideology that appeals to the aspirations of ordinary people who feel disrespected and forgotten. It offers them hope and it promises them respect. These "ordinary people" become the base of support for the populist leader. It is no wonder they come to adulate this leader, since they feel they finally have a champion who will fight for them.

There is value in recognizing the needs of a forgotten group of people, and populist leaders can be genuine in their concern. Pope Francis recognizes this, referencing "popular" leaders:

3. Pope Francis, *Fratelli Tutti*, 159.
4. Pope Francis, *Fratelli Tutti*, 155.

'Popular' leaders, those capable of interpreting the feelings and cultural dynamics of a people . . . [and] their efforts to unite and lead can become the basis of an enduring vision of transformation and growth that would also include making room for others in the pursuit of the common good.[5]

But the pope's key phrases are "making room for others," and "the pursuit of the common good," and unless the leader undertakes these deliberate pursuits, populism will more likely lead to division and polarization of a people.

We'll return to the populist's base of support, but first we assess the populist leaders themselves.

The Populist Leader

While populist leaders can genuinely care for the people in their base of support, the characteristics of many populist leaders across the world today suggest they commonly do not. Instead, they use and manipulate their base for their own personal and political benefit. Pope Francis references "an unhealthy populism" that occurs when:

individuals are able to exploit [others] for their own . . . personal advantage or continuing grip on power.[6]

For this reason, it is useful to consider the common characteristics of populist leaders. No two leaders are the same, though many of these characteristics apply, to various degrees, to all populist leaders.

First is the significance of the populist's ego, which is generally both oversized and fragile. Maintaining this ego can be the focal point of the populist's policies and practices. In this regard, everything becomes about the leader.

For example, crowd size is important, as large adoring crowds bolster the ego of the populist. These leaders may exaggerate or even lie about crowd size. They may compare their crowd sizes with those of other politicians, and they may proclaim, rather absurdly, that large crowds of people, such as victims seeking disaster assistance, are gathered in support of their leader. Once again, it is all about the leader.

---

5. Pope Francis, *Fratelli Tutti,* 159.
6. Pope Francis, *Fratelli Tutti,* 159.

Fragile egos require continual reassurance. Successes are exaggerated. Errors and failures are covered up and denied. Indeed, the populist may be truly incompetent, so that cover-ups are continual. Owners of fragile egos will lie, cheat, and steal to maintain these egos. They are obsessed by their need to "win." They "celebrate their presence" with bizarre photo-ops that most people consider, well, bizarre. Those with fragile egos will never truly meet the needs of the people of their base because they never truly care about them. Indeed, their own narcissism prevents them from doing so.

Populist leaders are often charismatic or cult-like figures. Besides being self-absorbed, they can be impulsive and mentally unstable. They are attracted to conspiracy theories, and they lie so constantly they believe their own falsehoods. They promise much and deliver little. They revel in inspirational slogans but fail to understand the intricacies of policy. They choose their advisers for loyalty over competence. They promise to improve the fortunes of their base but have no clear idea of what they mean by this.

Pope Francis observes that populist leaders often appeal to their base with claims of carnage and despair.

> The best way to dominate and gain control over people is to spread despair and discouragement.[7]

They then disparage their opponents and those they define as the "elite establishment," such that:

> Hyperbole, extremism, and polarization . . . become political tools . . . [in] a strategy of ridicule, suspicion and relentless criticism.[8]

Politics then becomes unhealthy and divisive:

> Political life . . . [is] aimed at discrediting others . . . [and] debate degenerates into a permanent state of disagreement and confrontation.[9]

Ultimately, populists can be racist.

> Instances of racism continue to shame us, for they show that our supposed social progress is not as real or definitive as we think.[10]

7. Pope Francis, *Fratelli Tutti,* 15.

8. Pope Francis, *Fratelli Tutti,* 15.

9. Pope Francis, *Fratelli Tutti,* 15.

10. Pope Francis, *Fratelli Tutti,* 20. The phrase, "Instances of racism," is misleading, as there is considerable evidence that racism is systemic in countries like the U.S. For example, see Brux, "Inequality and Racism."

The Base

We've recognized that populists like to present themselves as the voice of the "forgotten people." These "forgotten people" are the ones left behind by changing times and changing economies, and they feel ignored by others whose fortunes are rising. Once again, we recognize that "the forgotten people" become the populist's base of support, a group that is used and manipulated to achieve the goals of the leader. This is one well-established group of people we will consider more carefully in the context of the United States in Chapter 3.

The Establishment

Populists also charge an elite establishment with ignoring the needs of their base and looking down upon them. In some cases, these charges may be legitimate, and it is good for those who align with the establishment to be aware of the impact of their privilege on others less well endowed. But populists can also foster ill-will when none had existed, often using the ridicule and derision referenced by the pope to vilify the elite and polarize them from the populist's base. People in the elite establishment include previous leaders, competing politicians, and anyone who might be admired more widely than the populist leader. Members of the establishment often fall victim to the populist's insults, since the populist "must be" loved above all others. In other words, honorable people of the establishment can be treated dishonorably.

Perhaps the best single attempt to disparage "the establishment" comes in the form of Q-Anon, a rightwing conspiracy group that espouses the view that former President Trump is waging a secret war against elite Satan-worshipping pedophiles in government, business and the media. In particular, adherents believe a cabal of satanic cannibalistic traffickers and child sex abusers exists within Hollywood, the Democratic Party, and the so-called "deep state" within government. Expanding its presence through the use of social media, Q-Anon now has a large representation in Germany and Brazil, and has spread to the United Kingdom, Canada, Australia, and some seventy other countries. Among the central beliefs include racist views that Hillary Clinton, Barack Obama, and Joe Biden are all secretly working to hold down the Black population, that Black Lives Matter is a front to fund President Biden, that Democrats formed the Ku Klux Klan, and that Barack Obama is Satan himself and has armed North Korea with nuclear weapons. If some of this seems a bit too bizarre for you, consider the fact that two members of Congress, notably House Representatives Marjorie Taylor Greene and Lauren Boebert, were voted into office while promoting Q-Anon. Furthermore, the share of Americans who believe in the main tenets of the Q-Anon has increased from 14 percent in March 2021 to 18 percent in March 2022![11]

The Scapegoats

Aside from the "elite establishment" and the populist leader's base of support, we recognize a final group of people harmed by populism that we'll refer to as the "scapegoats." Populist leaders mislead and goad their base of support into fearing and even hating this group of people that the leader defines as the source of their misery. Populist leaders target the scapegoats, exaggerating their cultural differences and demeaning their characters. They create "a politics of grievance" among their base and "culture wars" between the base and culturally diverse populations. These culture wars exaggerate differences between the base and the scapegoats, and these scapegoats, often immigrants and people of color, are derided for their skin color, religion, and nationality. On the other hand, the populist's followers are generally white, and can include white evangelical Christians, white supremacists, and even white militant groups.

In these ways, populism degenerates into racism and bigotry. We will consider the three groups of populism's victims—the manipulated base, the honorable people of the establishment, and the scapegoated immigrants and people of color—in more detail shortly, but we first continue to describe the rightwing ideologies, specifically that of nationalism. Populism becomes even more disconcerting when combined with nationalism.

POPULISM AND NATIONALISM

Populist leaders are frequently nationalists, meaning they seemingly place their country and population groups within their country above the rest of the world. This "patriotism" can be genuine, though usually misguided; but

---

11. Huff, "Q-Anon Beliefs."

more likely, it is just another ploy for the populist leader to manipulate its base.

When populist leaders evoke nationalism, they encourage grudges against foreign countries. They may ridicule foreign leaders and foreign cultures. And they vehemently oppose immigration to the point where they lie about and denigrate would-be immigrants. They dwell on "illegals" and insist they are criminals. They place asylum-seekers and refugees in the same category as drug dealers and human traffickers, and they fail to acknowledge the reasons why immigrants flee their homes. Nationalistic populists degrade immigrant communities in their rallies and tweets, and they lie about jobs "stolen" by immigrants and violent perils encountered with them. They lack concern for global victims of oppression and disaster, often claiming rather oddly that the foreign population brought it on themselves. Indeed, they likely know little or nothing about these foreign populations. (Donald Trump, for example, wondered if Finland was part of Russia; and while running for Vice President, Sarah Palin believed Africa to be one country.)

Nationalistic populists generally oppose providing foreign aid, and they often claim that other countries are contributing less than they are. However, to deny foreign aid to desperate people is a short-lived victory for a nationalistic populist, whose own country's prosperity and security ultimately suffer as a result. Global organizations and agreements are treated with hostility because nationalistic populists believe that any policy benefiting one country must, by definition, be harming another. In other words, nationalistic populists see the world as a "zero-sum game," meaning there is only so much "good" in the world, whether this "good" refers to productive resources, consumer products, or various forms of wealth and money. More for one country means less for another, and populists claim their own country is losing. This is especially the case with policies and agreements promoted under previous leadership. The populist leader can then become the "savior" of its country by reversing the "damaging" previous practices.

But the world is not a zero-sum game. Global relations and agreements can create greater good for the entire world through cooperation and synergies that make all collaborating countries better off. Free trade agreements can achieve greater economic efficiencies, thereby leading to higher employment, output, and standards of living for people in all trading countries. Global agreements on climate change and nuclear restrictions are vital to saving the planet. Development of a vaccine against COVID-19 theoretically benefited the entire world.

Similarly, economists argue that refugees and immigrants bring enormous benefits to their host countries. They generate economic growth and job creation. Their younger average age means they will work for many years, paying taxes to support an aging domestic population while funding any services the immigrant family receives. The aging populations of the United States, Europe, China, and India make it imperative to expand local labor forces, and immigration is both a humanitarian and effective means of doing so. And, of course, immigrants bring vitality and diversity to communities and neighborhoods. We will return to this shortly.

Generous immigration policies are but one example of the benefits received through global cooperation and the harm that is done by disparaging it.

> Mutual assistance between countries proves enriching for each . . .
> We need to develop the awareness that nowadays we are either all saved together or no one is saved. Poverty, decadence and suffering in one part of the earth are a silent breeding ground for problems that will end up affecting the entire planet.[12]

Even if no benefits were gained by generous immigration and foreign aid policies, there is always a role for compassion, or as the pope says, for "gratuitousness." This is:

> the ability to do some things simply because they are good in themselves, without concern for personal gain or recompense.[13]

Pope Francis continues by saying:

> Gratuitousness makes it possible for us to welcome the stranger, even though this brings us no immediate tangible benefit . . . Life without fraternal gratuitousness becomes a form of frenetic commerce, in which we are constantly weighing up what we give and what we get back in return . . . Narrow forms of nationalism are an extreme expression of an inability to grasp the meaning of this gratuitousness.[14]

---

12. Pope Francis, *Fratelli Tutti,* 137.

13. Pope Francis, *Fratelli Tutti,* 139.

14. Pope Francis, *Fratelli Tutti,* 139–141.

Despite the enormous benefits of global cooperation, nationalistic populists fail to see them. In their zeal for their own nation's fortune, they also lack foresight and compassion for others in need.

Populism and nationalism are even more dangerous when combined with authoritarianism.

POPULISM AND AUTHORITARIANISM

Populist leaders have a natural tilt toward authoritarianism. This stems from their narcissism and desire for power. Authoritarianism is the opposite of democracy. It is associated with the breakdown of democratic institutions, such as a free press and an independent judicial system. It gives rise to assaults on democratic freedoms, such as the rights to free speech and peaceful protest. It purges voting rolls and delegitimizes elections in the minds of the authoritarian's base. Most importantly, it gives way to power by a strong central authority, who uses that power to do everything necessary to retain it.

Authoritarianism can be absolute and immediate, as when a military coup gives rise to a dictator. But it can also arise gradually, as it does when a leader creates fear and mistrust in one institution after another, breaking down norms, and obliterating freedoms. We are talking about basic freedoms of speech, religion, the right to peacefully protest and assemble, and the other rights and freedoms listed in our constitution. Authoritarianism can creep into existence and tolerance as people are lulled into accepting what once would have been unthinkable. This means that complacency and complicity help consolidate the power of authoritarian leaders. We know from recent history that authoritarian leaders can plan elaborate takeovers, working with their allies and supported by political parties too frightened or intimidated to speak out against them. The best examples since 2021 include the United States, Germany, and Brazil.[15] In these cases, the au-

---

15. The reference is to the U.S. on January 6, 2021, Germany in 2022, and Brazil in 2023. In the German case, members of a suspected far-right terrorist group called the Patriotic Union allegedly sought to reestablish a monarchist government in Germany in the tradition of the authoritarian German Reich. In Brazil, far right supporters of former President Jair Bolsonaro attempted a coup by storming the seats of political, judicial and legislative power. None of these coup attempts were successful.

thoritarian leader or group, even if failing to achieve the coup, seemingly gets away with the effort.[16]

THE VICTIMS OF POPULISM

We've identified (at least) three groups of people who fall victim to populist ideology, as well as to nationalism and authoritarianism. As a reminder, the first group consists of the members of the populist's base of support, especially when these people are used and manipulated solely for the benefit of the leader. Given populist leaders' ignorance of policy, their impulsiveness, their incompetence, and especially their narcissism, they are unlikely to achieve real benefits for the people in their base. Their supporters may well become worse off, such as the farmers who suffered from Donald Trump's tariffs. Supporters also suffer when convinced by the populist they should act out in violent or otherwise illegal ways, such as those convicted of crimes on January 6, 2021. They will spend many of their remaining days in prison.

The second group of victims is the elite establishment, which the populist treats with ridicule and condescension. Certainly, this can damage people's reputations and livelihoods. In the extreme, it can create such rage among members of the base that they pose a physical threat to the members of this so-called establishment. Indeed, anyone who exhibits opposition to the populist, or alternatively, achieves greater popularity than the populist, can face similar threats.

Finally, more than anyone else, the scapegoats who are blamed for the problems among the populist's base are stereotyped, vilified, and become the most visible contingent of populism's victims. They are frequently people of color and immigrants, and we will consider them in greater detail.

The Scapegoats

Populism's scapegoats are typically people of color and diverse cultures, and include Blacks, Hispanics, and Indigenous; Jews, Buddhists, Sikhs, and Muslims; and most notably, immigrants from almost anywhere on the planet. The pope tells us about the link to racism:

---

16. Thus far as I write this, Trump has not been penalized for his role in the insurrection, though many of the insurrectionists have been imprisoned.

racism is a virus that quickly mutates and, instead of disappearing, goes into hiding, and lurks in waiting.[17]

Except that today, racism is evident in full force.

The pope also goes on to address immigration:

> migration causes fear and alarm, often fomented and exploited for political purposes . . . [leading] to a xenophobic mentality, as people close in on themselves.[18]

Thus, the toxic combination of populism and nationalism is responsible for racism and xenophobia, which in turn are responsible for the wave of anti-immigration fervor across the globe. Millions of immigrants have fled their homes, seeking to escape poverty, climate disasters, and conflict zones around the world. These include asylum-seekers evading the ravages of climate change and the violence of drug dealers and gangs in Central and South America and the Caribbean who have surged to the U.S.-Mexican border. Others are fleeing war and conflict zones in Africa and the Middle East. The newest global asylum-seekers are those fleeing violence in Afghanistan and Ukraine.

While leaders of many countries have stepped up admirably to meet their shared responsibility for admitting asylum-seekers and refugees, many of the world's nationalistic populist's instead disparage the immigrants and exaggerate the irrational fears of their citizens. According to Pope Francis, these leaders:

> seek popularity by appealing to the basest and most selfish inclinations of certain sectors of the population [their base].[19]

Often fraught with racism, nationalistic populists treat immigrants with derision and falsely depict them as criminals and terrorists. They lie about the impact of immigrants on the domestic economy, and they create a false specter of joblessness and overrun schools. In these ways, nationalist populists create an exaggerated fear of immigrants and unwarranted opposition to their immigration. In reverting to racism, xenophobia, and deceit, the populist appeals to the basest and most selfish inclinations referenced by the pope. Ultimately, Pope Francis concludes that:

---

17. Pope Francis, *Fratelli Tutti*, 97.
18. Pope Francis, *Fratelli Tutti*, 39.
19. Pope Francis, *Fratelli Tutti*, 159.

one part of humanity . . . sees its own dignity denied, scorned or trampled upon, and its fundamental rights discarded or violated.[20]

It's hard to imagine the level of contempt directed towards those facing violence and devastation sufficient to force them from their homelands. Our normal human responses of compassion and empathy are obliterated by the fears and lies incited by populist leaders. Social media magnifies the tweets and retweets such that the bombardment of hateful rage demands attention and evokes a hostile response. What was once said in whispers is now spoken loudly. This is lamented by the pope:

> Things that until a few years ago could not be said by anyone without risking the loss of universal respect can now be said with impunity, and in the crudest of terms, even by some political figures . . . [There is a] spread of fake news and false information, fomenting prejudice and hate.[21]

Examples of racist language are not difficult to find among U.S. politicians and elsewhere. By Biden's mid-presidency, examples of racism were flourishing. Some of these include the following:

- Sen. Tommy Tuberville suggested at a rally in Nevada that Black people are criminals. This occurred during a debate over whether to provide reparations to the descendants of enslaved people, when Tuberville charged that Democrats were "pro-crime." "They want crime because they want to take over what you got. They want to control what you have. They want reparations because they think the people that do the crime are owed that." Pay close attention to that very last sentence. In plain English, reparations would go to Blacks and Blacks are the criminals.[22]

- A slightly more subtle ad paid for by the conservative Club for Growth political action committee features the mug shot of a Black sex offender and blames candidate North Carolina Supreme Court Justice Cheri Beasley for his being unmonitored.[23] (This may remind you of the 1988 George H.W. Bush presidential campaign ad featuring a mug shot of Black offender Willie Horton.) This type of ad has become a

---

20. Pope Francis, *Fratelli Tutti*, 22.

21. Pope Francis, *Fratelli Tutti*, 45.

22. Chatelain, "Tuberville, Greene Slammed."

23. Specht, "Fact Check."

classic example of "dog whistle" racism in politics, with similar ads featuring mug shots of Black defendants in Wisconsin and North Carolina. Some suggest that the subtle racism that arouses anger and fear in these ads is more effective than overtly racist messages.

- Kanye West, now called Ye, tweeted that he wanted to go "death con 3" on "JEWISH PEOPLE,"[24] an apparent reference to Defcon, the U.S. military defense readiness system. Instagram and Twitter removed his posts, though Ye was featured on conservative Fox News host Tucker Carlson's show. Circumstances deteriorated weeks later when Ye and his companion, Nick Fuentes, a well-known neo-Nazi and white supremacist, joined Trump for dinner at Mar-a-Lago.

- The Nazi curriculum for a group of Ohio's home-schooled children includes "ready-made lesson plans", some of which are history lessons that praise the Confederate general Robert E. Lee as a "grand role model for young, white men" and denigrate Martin Luther King Jr as "the antithesis of our civilization and our people". Material states that Black people are inferior to whites.[25]

- As a final example, there is a growing hysteria among rightwing politicians across the world about "replacement theory," in which they argue that foreign cultures and people of color threaten the "purity" of their own white culture. Some go further, claiming the genetics of foreigners and people of color threaten the purity of their own "superior" genes. Rising numbers of immigrants and relatively high birthrates among people of color do create the potential for a new majority consisting of a non-white population, whom the populists fear will vote "against them" and leave the base behind.[26]

Consider just two more examples of the scripting of U.S. rightwing politicians using their own versions of replacement theory.

- At a Trump rally in Arizona, Representative Margorie Taylor Greene stated that: "Joe Biden's five million illegal aliens are on the verge of

24. Cramer and Kampeas, "Kanye West's Vow."

25. Gabbatt, "Outrage Over Alleged Nazi Homeschooling."

26. It is difficult to reference people of color, since according to the Census Bureau, "Hispanic" is an ethnicity and not a race. Hispanics may be of any race and the majority is white. On the other hand, the terms white, Black, Indigenous, and Asian refer to races. We simplify in this book by referring to all Hispanics as people of color. We also follow the practice of capitalizing races when the term includes a cultural context, such as Black.

replacing you, replacing your jobs and replacing your kids in school and coming from all over the world, they're also replacing your culture."[27]

- Whereas Greene was referencing immigrants, there is a clear link between her statement and the 2017 Charlottesville debacle, when Trump claimed there were "very fine people" on both sides, including the side that chanted, "Jews will not replace us!" Apparently, a racist chant by white supremacist neo-Nazis has made its way into acceptable Republican commentary.

Populists insist the replacement is intentional by those on the left, who are sympathetic to racial and immigrant causes. Hence, Democrats are demonized in the same way as the scapegoats. Nevertheless, prejudice and hate violate the dictums of the faith of American president Biden who is battling for the soul of the nation. They are anathema to this same religion espoused by the pope. As such, Pope Francis states that populism:

> sets certain political preferences above deep convictions of our faith: the inalienable dignity of each human person regardless of origin, race or religion, and the supreme law of fraternal love.[28]

To be clear—not all populists are racist. Not all populists are bigoted. And not all populists disparage their fellow human beings. Indeed, there are populists on the left as well as on the right, who neglect the advice of economists to support populist messages like protectionism over free trade.[29]

But, the nature of populism, especially across our world today, has more of a conservative bent. This means that scapegoats are essential to the popularity of populist leaders amid their bases of support. Someone must be held accountable for the troubles afflicting the base. When this base consists of white, Christian, and European-descended people, the natural scapegoats will be people of color, non-Christian religions, and non-European descent. Populism exploits cultural differences, appeals to white people that include white supremacists, and tilts towards authoritarianism.

---

27. Chatelain, "Tuberville, Greene Slammed."

28. Pope Francis, *Fratelli Tutti*, 39.

29. President Biden, for example, uses populist terminology when calling for programs to purchase products made in America. Economists believe this kind of protectionism can create more harm than good.

The alliance of populism with nationalism assures that immigrants will be primary scapegoats, along people of color.

Pope Francis recognizes opposition to immigrants most vividly in the "construction of walls."

The Walls

Populists are in the business of building walls, which the pope refers to as:

> a culture of walls . . . walls in the heart, walls on the land, in order to prevent this encounter with other cultures, with other people.[30]

The pope further explains that:

> There is a kind of "local" narcissism . . . born of a certain insecurity and fear of the other that leads to rejection and the desire to erect walls for self-defense.[31]

And the walls most literal are the physical border walls demanded by nationalistic populists and intended to keep out immigrants, such that "an influx of migrants is to be prevented at all costs."[32] We will return to immigrants and other people of color as the principal scapegoats, as well as the primary victims, of populism. We will also again refer to "the walls" in the context of Trump's vicious attitude toward immigrants.

WHITE CHRISTIAN NATIONALISM

Religious nationalism, and specifically white Christian nationalism, is an ideology that goes beyond mere nationalism that places one's own country and people above all others. It adds the dimension of religion. In the case of Christianity, it asserts that Christianity should be at the heart of patriotism and civic life. For white Christian nationalists, it also means that true patriots are white, culturally conservative, and natural born citizens.

In the United States, Christian nationalism appeals primarily to Protestants. This stems from a backdrop of early 1600's government discrimination against Catholics, who were banned from the colonies, and Quakers, who were hanged. Phrases like "God is on America's side" are

30. Pope Francis, *Fratelli Tutti*, 27.

31. Pope Francis, *Fratelli Tutti*, 146.

32. Pope Francis, *Fratelli Tutti*, 37.

common among Christian nationalists, and there is a view that God has given America a special role in history. Adherents support school prayer, public religious displays, and private religious schools funded by government vouchers that would otherwise provide funding for our public school system. Of course, these refer to Christian prayers, Christian displays, and Christian schools.[33]

Multiple rightwing American politicians have placed themselves in the company of U.S. Christian nationalists. For example, Representative Margorie Taylor Greene uses biblical phrases in her speech, Representative Madison Cawthorn spoke of a "spiritual battle" on Capitol Hill, and Lieutenant Governor Janet McGeachin was photographed holding a bible and a gun and saying, "God calls us to pick up the sword and fight." After a victory for Pennsylvania Senator Doug Mastriano, his Facebook page had the words, "Praise Jesus!" and "Thank you Father God!!!" Florida Governor Ron DeSantis said in a recent speech, "Put on the full armor of God. Stand firm against the Left's schemes."[34]

One more example displays Christian nationalism to a shocking degree. The quotation is from a message sent by Representative Rick Allen to Donald Trump's Chief of Staff Mark Meadows in the days following the January 6 insurrection.

> Mark, please know that I have prayed for President Trump, his family, for you and the entire Administration. Our Nation is at war, it is a Spiritual War at the highest level. This is not a war that can be fought conventionally, this is God's battle, and He has used President Trump in a powerful way to expose the deceit, lies and hypocrisy of the enemy. The Trump family and all of us have paid a heavy price to be used by the Father but the War is just beginning. We have had a major setback and people are taking sides, and my plea to my fellow believers who want to cut and run [because of January 6] is judge not less you be judged, we have all fallen short of the Glory of Almighty God. What I heard during my prayers is the Trump family and the Administration need to be surrounded by those great Pastors and Evangelicals who have snd

---

33. Vouchers are certificates that provide government payments, in this case for children receiving private education. The financing for the voucher comes from the pool of money otherwise used for public education. Thus, harm is done to public schools that lose funding and are most likely to be attended by non-white and poorer students. We will address vouchers again later in the book.

34. Brechtel, "Madison Cawthorn Called Out;" Miller, "Idaho Lieutenant Governor;" Mastriano, "Praise Jesus;" Saavedra, "DeSantis: Take A Stand."

[sic] continue to love and support them. President Trump needs to be ministered to, he needs the love that only Jesus Christ offers! This is his opportunity to confess that he can no longer fight this battle alone, he must give it to Christ and Gid [sic] almighty will show him the way to victory. I will continue to pray for all of you, please let me know how I can help.[35]

Okay, so this is "God's battle" and "He has used President Trump in a powerful way to expose the deceit, lies and hypocrisy of the enemy." Who is the enemy? How has this enemy lied and about what? What is the "deceit" and "hypocrisy"?

I can't pretend to know just what Representative Allen was writing about. I can guess that the enemy is the "left" and the lies pertain to Biden's election win and the left's "woke" agenda. The "woke" worldview is not all that radical: it acknowledges the true history of colonialism, slavery, and genocide against Indigenous and other native people. We know these to be factual. Perhaps the problem for Representative Allen is that devout American Christians were among those who killed Native Americans and enslaved Black people. Perhaps it is more palatable for them to deny it.

It is notable that on January 6, protesters at the Capitol carried a plethora of Christian jewelry, art, flags, and signs; and the words "Jesus," "Christ," and "Christianity" were written and spoken everywhere, including on the gallows put up for the purpose of hanging Mike Pence. Despite the violence, injury, and death caused by the insurrection, most Republican politicians have not spoken out against it, and the Republican National Committee referred to it as "legitimate discourse". The comingling of violence and Christianity should cause us to pause.

White Christian nationalism plays a key role in politics. It swims amidst the ideologies of populism, nationalism, authoritarianism, and even capitalism. And while it receives the approval of populists in the mode of Donald Trump, it is opposed by the likes of Pope Francis and President Biden. Other forms of religious nationalism occur around the world. The best example may be Hindu nationalism, which we will address later in the book.

Now we turn to our final ideology, which is capitalism.

35. Pierce, "Georgia, Come and Collect."

CAPITALISM

Capitalism is both an ideology and an economic system. Its two basic characteristics are these: 1) the means of production (factories, offices, machinery, tools, and so on) are owned primarily by the private sector, and 2) the economic decisions are made principally by private individuals and businesses. Hence, for example, prices are determined by the interactions of private consumers and private businesses in free markets. Consumers decide what and how much to buy at various prices, and businesses decide what and how much to sell. If too many goods are available (a surplus), the tendency is for the price to fall. If too few goods are available (a shortage), the price tends to rise. Either way, a market equilibrium price with no surpluses or shortages is achieved.

Furthermore, consumers try to maximize their well-being and businesses seek to maximize their profits. Workers decide whether to work at market wages and business firms decide whether to hire large amounts of labor relative to capital or vice versa, depending on the relative market wages for labor and the prices of capital. A critical objective of capitalism is efficiency, and there is an emphasis on economic growth, which may or may not trickle down to those at the bottom. A great deal of history reveals it does not.

Notably, these characteristics mean a minimal role for government. All economists do recognize a role for government in addressing market failures, such as the need for public goods like parks and libraries, the problem of pollution, and the tendency toward market power and economic instability (inflation and recession) in a capitalist economy. But, for the most part, economists on the right believe that too much government intervention detracts from the efficiency and productivity of the capitalist economy.

The opposite of capitalism is socialism, an economic system with these characteristics: 1) the means of production are owned primarily by the public sector; that is, the government, and 2) the economic decisions are principally made by the public sector. Hence, decisions such as pricing are made by the government. The government determines what businesses will produce and how they will produce them. The government controls the distribution of goods and services and the employment of labor. Whereas efficiency is the main goal of capitalism, equity is considered the primary goal of socialism. Equity simply means fairness, and fairness may require the intervention of government in providing a widespread safety net that assures the well-being of all its citizens.

While socialism and capitalism are opposites, most economies range somewhere in-between. Some countries have greater government involvement, such as the "welfare states" of several European countries; and others pride themselves on minimal government, such as the United States. Those who extol socialism may look down on any country that permits its people to go hungry and homeless; whereas defenders of capitalism largely believe that the profit motive and other economic incentives assure hard work and effort and therefore high productivity. They justify exorbitant wealth by explaining "the wealthy work hard for their money." Given the high degree of inequality in the United States, along with the fact that the poorest are often the hardest workers, thoughtful people question this justification for excessive profits, income, and wealth, which have often been achieved on the backs of the poor.

Bear in mind that capitalism and socialism define economic systems, whereas democracy and authoritarianism are political systems. Any political system, from democracy to authoritarian, can be associated with any economic system, from capitalism to socialism. And while capitalism and socialism refer to economic systems, they can also be considered as ideologies (just as democracy and authoritarianism are also ideologies). The religious fervor with which some promote either capitalism or socialism attests to that.

The pope himself is wary of capitalism. He sees it as creating inequality and poverty.

> Some economic rules have proved effective for growth, but not for integral human development. Wealth has increased, but together with inequality, with the result that "new forms of poverty are emerging."[36]

The pope also warns of the dangers of consumerism associated with capitalism:

> Nor should we naively refuse to recognize that "obsession with a consumerist lifestyle, above all when few people are capable of maintaining it, can only lead to violence and mutual destruction. . . . The notion of 'every man for himself' will rapidly degenerate into a free-for-all that would prove worse than any pandemic.[37]

---

36. Pope Francis, *Fratelli Tutti*, 21.
37. Pope Francis, *Fratelli Tutti*, 36.

And perhaps most critically, the pope is concerned about unbridled capitalism's exploitation of labor and the creation of poverty associated with that.

> This way of discarding others can take a variety of forms, such as an obsession with reducing labour costs with no concern for its grave consequences, since the unemployment that it directly generates leads to the expansion of poverty.[38]

Like populism, unrestrained capitalism can discard and disregard others. These include not just exploited consumers and workers, and not just the poor and struggling, but other victims as well. These include the casualties of racism. According to the pope,

> a readiness to discard others finds expression in vicious attitudes that we thought long past, such as racism, which retreats underground only to keep reemerging.[39]

Whereas Pope Francis recognizes "instances" of racism, as referenced earlier, he also seems to recognize its systemic nature, one that can go underground and retreat and later reemerge.

Finally, notice the use of phrases like "unbridled capitalism" and "unrestrained capitalism," Here again we encounter the role of government. Capitalism has very different outcomes when the government provides a generous safety net for the population, regulates against the exploitation of labor, and controls market power. When conservative policies that minimize the role of government in the economy take hold, then our unrestrained capitalist system can become very exploitative indeed.

WHAT DOES THIS MEAN FOR US?

So far, we've considered the ideologies of populism, nationalism, authoritarianism, and capitalism. If you are struggling to imagine how these various ideologies operate in our actual world, you will no doubt find it easier to understand them in the context of real-world examples. Since Donald Trump is the world's best-known populist, we will consider him first in the next chapter and then later address other world leaders with similar proclivities.

38. Pope Francis, *Fratelli Tutti*, 20.
39. Pope Francis, *Fratelli Tutti*, 20.

The pope makes it clear he is speaking to all of us—not just Catholics, not just Christians, and not just people of faith. He states:

> Although I have written . . . from the Christian convictions that inspire and sustain me, I have sought to make this reflection an invitation to dialogue among all people of good will.[40]

Remarkably, we will see throughout this book the intersection of religion and politics. The religious elements encompass a range of views from white supremacist Christian nationalism to Joe Biden's quest for the soul of the nation. We have noted and watched as a non-religious populist president stood for a photo-op while holding someone's bible at someone else's church. We have seen churches defiled with militarism and learned of mosques and synagogues threatened and assaulted with bombs. We've read of mass shootings in Black churches and Muslim mosques. We are aware of hate speech and anti-Semitism towards people of the Jewish faith. Religion, for better or worse, is implicit in our politics.

The pope calls us all to care for the victims of populism, including the forgotten people of the populist's base, the honorable yet dishonored people among the establishment, and the scapegoats who are feared, lied about, and blamed for the problems faced by the base. In one way or another, these people are all discarded by populism. The pope also calls us to care for those exploited by unrestrained capitalism in their consumerism and their labor, and especially those who are poor, immigrants, or victims of racism. He refers to all of the victims of populism and capitalism as "the marginalized," and if we must care for them, we must first know who they are. We must learn their stories. We must "visit them" in some manner, bringing our compassion and healing. And we must love them. After all, *Fratelli Tutti,* sisters and brothers all, is all about familial love. And we are now in the battle for the soul of a nation.

QUESTIONS FOR DISCUSSION

1. Do you agree with the descriptions and characterization of populist leaders?

2. Do you believe that populist leaders deliberately polarize their base from the establishment? Does the establishment truly disparage the base?

40. Pope Francis, *Fratelli Tutti,* 6.

3. Who are the scapegoats of the populist leader?

4. How do populist leaders vilify the scapegoats, leaving them discarded and marginalized?

5. What is the role of racism amidst populism, nationalism, and unrestrained capitalism?

6. Is the world a zero-sum game? Explain.

7. What do you think of white Christian nationalism? Are you troubled by its link to violence? To racism?

8. What do you think of Q-Anon? Why do so many people believe in what has been shown to be a conspiracy theory?

Chapter 3

Trumpism
Populism, Nationalism, and Authoritarianism

FRATELLI TUTTI WAS PUBLISHED in October 2020, proving itself to be profoundly prescient of the times. Pope Francis wrote amid a global spread of populism, climate change, and COVID-19, and he used his various encyclicals to pronounce his concerns about all.

Ironically, *Fratelli Tutti* also serves as a backdrop to the November 2020 election defeat of former U.S. President Donald Trump,[1] who has been the modern world's most visible example of a populist leader. *Fratelli Tutti* presents us with an opportunity to assess Trump's presidency and reelection defeat in one country and to consider the broader appeal of populism across the Republican party in the United States today and in other countries across the world. We address the United States in this chapter and other nations in the next.

The point is not to disparage Trump, though it is true that will take place. The point is to identify the elements of his populism, nationalism, and authoritarianism in real-life terms and to examine their impact on real-world people.

TRUMP'S POPULISM

Trump defined populism with a phrase:

---

1. Trump's quotations are referenced by date of quotation or date reported.

Make America Great Again (MAGA)

Think about this. Trump's campaign slogan, emblazoned on the hats of Trump supporters everywhere, presumes that America isn't great now, but at one time it was. Trump's populist message to his base of support was that they too had once been great, but some force of time left them unneeded, disrespected, and disregarded. He promised he would right their wrongs and restore them to greatness.

Trump's Inaugural Address

Trump began his presidency in the manner of a populist: he created a portrait of America as a country deep in despair, intimating that some segments of the nation's population were being harmed by others. His inaugural speech became known as his "American carnage speech."

> But for too many of our citizens, a different reality exists: Mothers and children trapped in poverty in our inner cities; rusted-out factories scattered like tombstones across the landscape of our nation; an education system, flush with cash, but which leaves our young and beautiful students deprived of knowledge; and the crime and gangs and drugs that have stolen too many lives and robbed our country of so much unrealized potential. This American carnage stops right here and stops right now.[2]

Oddly enough, given this speech, Trump was entirely uninterested in the problems of poverty of women and their children, our failing infrastructure, the inadequacy of our educational system, and so many other issues affecting the well-being of Americans. And ironically, Trump's reference to "American carnage" would eventually be used against him. The July 2022 statement of Representative Jamie Raskin of the January 6 Congressional Committee referenced Trump and the 2021 insurrection by saying:

> American carnage turned out to be an excellent prophecy of what his [Trump's] rage would come to visit on our people.[3]

We will return to this thought.

Other parts of Trump's inaugural address embodied the very essence of populism. He spoke to the forgotten Americans, recognizing their

2. Trump, "Inaugural Address," Jan 20, 2017.
3. Raskin, "American Carnage."

grievances toward a Washington elite and promising to restore their status. He said,

> Today . . . we are transferring power from Washington, D.C. and giving it back to you, the American People.[4]

Trump went on to describe the "elite establishment" and how this elite had treated the common people.

> For too long, a small group in our nation's Capital has reaped the rewards of government while the people have borne the cost. Washington flourished—but the people did not share in its wealth. Politicians prospered—but the jobs left, and the factories closed. The establishment protected itself, but not the citizens of our country.[5]

Then Trump celebrated this new moment for "the people":

> That all changes—starting right here, and right now, because this moment is your moment: it belongs to you . . . This is your day. This is your celebration . . . January 20th, 2017, will be remembered as the day the people became the rulers of this nation again.[6]

Finally, and most importantly, Trump promised "the people" they would never again be forgotten. They would be respected, and they would be listened to.

> The forgotten men and women of our country will be forgotten no longer. Everyone is listening to you now . . . You will never be ignored again. Your voice, your hopes, and your dreams, will define our American destiny. And your courage and goodness and love will forever guide us along the way. Together, We Will Make America Strong Again. We Will Make America Wealthy Again. We Will Make America Proud Again. We Will Make America Safe Again. And, Yes, Together, We Will Make America Great Again.[7]

These forgotten men and women were the base of support for Donald Trump, just as forgotten men and women form the base of support for populist leaders everywhere. We will address both the base and the "elite establishment" more extensively shortly.

4. Trump, "Inaugural Address," Jan 20, 2017.
5. Trump, "Inaugural Address," Jan 20, 2017.
6. Trump, "Inaugural Address," Jan 20, 2017.
7. Trump, "Inaugural Address," Jan 20, 2017.

Trump's Ego

Trump's single most identifying feature is his outsized ego. He needs to take center stage, whether it is gliding down a golden elevator to announce his candidacy or pushing aside the prime minister of Montenegro at a NATO meeting to move to the front of a group of leaders.

Trump's Ceremonies

As such, Trump was visibly impressed by foreign leaders who live lavish lifestyles amid jewels and gold, such as King Salman and the Crown Prince Mohammed of Saudi Arabia. Despite his election promise to disavow Saudi Arabia for its human rights abuses, Trump chose this country for the first overseas trip of his presidency. The Saudis turned this visit into an extravaganza, projecting giant American and Saudi flags on the side of a luxury hotel, hanging American flags on lampposts along strips of highway, and transforming the capital city into a showcase of American culture. The Saudi Harley-Davidson club held an alcohol-free biker rally and country music singer Toby Keith performed for a full house of Saudi fans, all of them men. Most importantly, Trump was a guest of the luxurious palace. The Saudi's recognized Trump's passion for drama when they gathered Trump, King Salman, and Egypt's Abdel Fattah El-Sisi for a sword dance, with the three ultimately laying their hands on a glowing orb for a photo-op.

The Saudi intention was to seek cozy ties with America, and the lavish attention they paid to Trump paid off for them throughout Trump's presidency. He supported Saudi Arabia and others when they imposed a blockade on Qatar. He lifted restrictions on weapons sales to Saudi Arabia, despite the country's long record of bombing and killing civilians in Yemen. And ultimately, Trump defended the Crown Prince Mohammed after he approved the 2018 killing of Saudi journalist and *Washington Post* columnist Jamal Khashoggi, whose body was dismembered (and still not entirely found).

Trump was attracted to other forms of pomp and circumstance as well. He longed for a repeat of the military extravaganza he experienced as a guest of President Emmanuel Macron on France's Bastille Day. He marveled at this show of military might and returned home to tell the U.S. military to do this for him. (They said no.) He was similarly impressed when, during a visit to China, massive military parades and troop displays were held in his honor. Trump's attraction to displays of military might was likely a forewarning of his authoritarian tendencies.

Trump's Photo-Ops

As revealed in Saudi Arabia and in Washington, D.C., Trump loved photo-ops, even when they were strange and inappropriate. We noted the example of when, in the wake of George Floyd's killing by Minneapolis police and largely peaceful Black Lives Matter demonstrations in Washington, D.C., Trump ordered police and the National Guard to use pepper balls, flash-bang grenades, and smoke canisters to clear a route for him through the demonstrators. Several other officials, including the Secretary of Defense, the Chair of the Joint Chiefs of Staff, the Attorney General, the National Security Adviser, and daughter Ivanka and Jared Kushner, joined Trump as he walked up to St. John's Episcopal Church in D.C.[8] There, Trump held up someone's bible, spoke about law and order, and was photographed.

Bishop Mariann Edgar Budde, who oversees St. John's Church, was furious. She tweeted that Trump:

> just used a Bible and a church of my diocese as a backdrop for a message antithetical to the teachings of Jesus and everything that our church stands for . . . The President did not come to pray; he did not lament the death of George Floyd or acknowledge the collective agony of people of color in our nation. He did not attempt to heal or bring calm to our troubled land.[9]

These remarks reveal that despite Trump's appeal to rightwing white evangelical Christians, he did not impress those who followed the social gospel as espoused by Bishop Edgar Budde (nor, for that matter, Pope Francis and President Biden). Trump seemingly had no inkling that his photo-op would be considered insincere and out-of-place for a man who rarely attended church.

Another rather odd and inappropriate photo-op took place after Trump returned home from Walter Reed Hospital after a bout with COVID-19. Still contagious, he came back to the White House, walked up the south portico staircase, stopped in front of an illuminated entrance

8. Secretary of Defense Mark Esper, Chair of the Joint Chiefs of Staff Mike Milley, Attorney General Bill Barr, National Security Adviser Robert O'Brien, and daughter Ivanka and Jared Kushner.

9. Chappell, "He Did Not Pray."

with four U.S. flags, and ceremoniously removed his mask while posing for cameras. Moments later, after walking inside the building, he re-emerged for a film shoot, which he placed on Twitter along with some bizarre advice about COVID-19:

> Don't let it dominate you. Don't be afraid of it. You're gonna beat it. We have the best medical equipment. We have the best medicines, all developed recently . . . Nobody that's a leader would not do what I did. And I know there's a risk, there's a danger, but that's OK. And now I'm better and maybe I'm immune—I don't know! But don't let it dominate your lives. Get out there. Be careful.[10]

Health practitioners were outraged over Trump's cavalier attitude toward COVID-19. His willingness to risk the health of his support staff, including housekeepers, janitors, and his Secret Service detail, was a cause for fury. Joe Lockhart, a former White House press secretary under Bill Clinton, said it most bluntly:

> This Presidency has turned grotesque. The President is a super-spreader who thinks he's immune and doesn't care how many he kills—as long as the camera gets his good side.[11]

Trump's Bragging

Trump's ego was not just large but was also quite fragile. He felt a constant need to gloat about what he perceived to be his wonderful qualities. The strangest example was Trump's oft-repeated statement, "I am a stable genius." Not many people brag about being a genius, and those who do are unlikely to emphasize their mental stability at the same time. It is not something a normal person would say, repeatedly, and often.

Trump referred to himself as a "stable genius" in January 2018 in response to concerns that he wasn't mentally fit for office. He repeated the phrase in May 2020 when House Speaker Nancy Pelosi expressed her hope "for an intervention" for Trump and conveyed concerns about his well-being after he abruptly left a meeting with Democrats. Another example was during the 2020 Democratic primary election campaign for president, when Trump compared himself to the leading Democrats for the position:

10. Trump, Oct 5, 2020, in Smith, et al., "Contagious Trump Removes Mask."
11. Lockhart, in Smith, et al., "It's Grotesque."

Actually, throughout my life, my two greatest assets have been mental stability and being, like, really smart . . . Being elected president on my first try should qualify as not smart, but genius . . . and a very stable genius at that![12]

Not only did Trump brag about his genius, but he insisted he wasn't demented—hence the very awkward video of him slowly and hesitantly reciting the answers he gave during an abbreviated medical assessment of his mental acuity. Many mental health professionals found the story quite amusing, but Trump was clearly proud of himself for slowly providing the minimally correct answers.

"Stable genius" is just one of the many boasts made by Trump. Others include the following.

- "I'm intelligent. Some people would say I'm very, very, very intelligent."[13]

- "Sorry losers and haters, but my IQ is one of the highest—and you all know it"[14]

- "I'm the most successful person ever to run for the presidency, by far. Nobody's ever been more successful than me. I'm the most successful person ever to run."[15]

- "I say, not in a braggadocios way, I've made billions and billions of dollars dealing with people all around the world."[16]

- "To be blunt, people would vote for me. They just would. Why? Maybe because I'm so good looking."[17]

- "All of the women on *The Apprentice* flirted with me—consciously or unconsciously. That's to be expected."[18]

12. Trump, Oct 6, 2020, "A Very Stable Genius," in Raphelson, "A Very Stable Genius."

13. Trump, Mar 4, 2020 , "Some People Would Say," in Kruse, "The 199 Most Donald Trump Things."

14. Trump, Sep 5, 2013, "Sorry Losers," in Useem, "What Does Donald Trump Really Want?"

15. Trump, Feb 6, 2015, "Most Successful," in Cillizza, "Donald Trump's Emperor."

16. Trump, Sep 16, 2020, "I've Made Billions," in Alice, "84 Most Outrageous."

17. Trump, Sep 19, 1999, "To Be Blunt," in Alice, "84 Most Outrageous."

18. Trump, Oct 8, 2016, "All the Women," in Alice, "84 Most Outrageous."

- [My] "successful career" as a politician, businessman, and television personality "would qualify as not smart, but genius … and a very stable genius at that!"[19]

We could go on, as this is not the complete set of Trump's "genius-type" statements, but the point has been made.

Trump's Crowd Size

A fragile ego might require luxurious surroundings, military parades, photo-ops, and plenty of bragging, but Trump needed something more. He needed crowd size.

Trump's was especially obsessed with crowd size on the day of his inauguration, an obsession that erupted into a contentious debate between his press staff and the reporters covering the event. Trump forced then-White House press secretary, Sean Spicer, to go in front of reporters and assert it had been "the largest audience to ever witness an inauguration, period, both in person and around the globe."[20] That, of course, was patently untrue. And unfortunately for Spicer, he knew, as did everyone else, that Trump's crowd size was considerably smaller than that of former President Barak Obama. The evidence was in all the photos circulated at the time.

Trump had plenty of inappropriate things to say to crowds, especially when speaking to survivors of hurricanes and other disasters. After Hurricane Maria in Puerto Rico in 2017, Trump disparaged local leaders and threw paper towels into a crowd of victims, establishing a memorable but not very authentic expression of presidential concern. To a group of Texas hurricane survivors, Trump boasted, "What a crowd, what a turnout."[21] And in the wake of the mass shooting in El Paso, Trump reminisced to a group of first responders and hospital officials about an earlier speech he had made:

> I was here three months ago. That place was packed . . . That was some crowd.[22]

Perhaps Trump's most egregious effort to amplify crowd size occurred during the "Stop the Steal" rally on January 6, 2021, the day of the

19. Trump, Dec 27, 2022, "A Very Stable Genius," in Alice, "84 Most Outrageous."

20. Hunt, "Trump's Inauguration Crowd."

21. Trump, Aug 29, 2017, "What a Crowd," in Bradshaw, "What a Crowd."

22. Trump, Aug 8, 2019, "That Place Was Packed," in Chute, et al., "Everything We Know."

insurrection. Trump struggled with aides to permit armed people through the magnetometers so the crowd would look as full as possible in the photographs. According to Cassidy Hutchinson, a former aide to Trump White House chief of staff Mark Meadows and speaking to the January 6 committee, "He was very concerned about the shot, the photograph we would get."[23] Trump later bragged that it "was the largest crowd that I have ever spoken to . . . that was a crowd where there was unbelievable love and patriotism in the air."[24] (He repeated his claim about the crowd being the biggest crowd he had ever spoken to no fewer than three times.)

One last example is especially galling for those who admire Dr. Martin Luther King Jr. In a speech to a socially conservative group, Trump lied about the crowd size he had drawn for a July Fourth speech, saying it was larger than Reverend King's "I have a dream" address.

> And Dr. King gave a speech and it was great . . . They showed the picture and it was massive . . . They said it was a million people . . . Then I gave my speech and they showed the same thing . . . My pictures were exactly the same, but the people were slightly closer together. They were more compact . . . There were more people, they were tighter together if you look at it.[25]

Trump's odd fixation on crowd size has not gone unnoticed. CNN's Chris Cillizza's felt compelled to comment: "Donald Trump's crowd size obsession explains his entire presidency."[26] This is, at least in part, quite true. Add in the photo-ops and strange bragging rights, and we see that crowd size is just one of multiple factors displaying the former president's ego, one that seemingly motivated his every word and action. The same is true of his denials and his lies.

Trump's Denials

On the one hand, Trump likes to brag. On the other hand, he denies his failures. Trump is especially wont to lie about or cover up his mistakes. One of his most sensational lies involved the "sharpie affair." It began with

23. Hutchinson (Jan 6 Committee), in Wong, "Cassidy Hutchinson's."

24. Trump, Jul 11, 2021, "There Was Unbelievable Love," in Goertzen, "There Was a Lot of Love."

25. Trump, Jun 17, 2022, "There Were More People," in Cillizza," "Donald Trump's Crowd Size Obsession."

26. Cillizza, "Donald Trump's Crowd Size Obsession."

an innocent, though erroneous, tweet from the president, warning that Alabama was in the path of the deadly Hurricane Dorian. It was not. But rather than admit a mistake, Trump spent the next five days defending his position and even drawing an arrow on a televised map of the storm path to force it through Alabama. And he did it all with a "Sharpie pen."

Trump's Lies

Trump's denial of a storm path was nothing in comparison to a presidential campaign and a four-year presidency filled with lies to the American public. He lied about former President Obama's birthplace. He lied about COVID-19. He lied about immigrants. He lied about Russia, and he lied about Ukraine. And ultimately, of course, he told the "big lie," that his reelection was stolen and that he indeed was the winner. He lied to the point that fact-checkers ran an excellent business. For example, by January 24, 2021, the *Washington Post* reported 30,575 false or misleading claims by Trump over the prior four years.[27] Said presidential historian Michael Beschloss, "I have never seen a president in American history who has lied so continuously and so outrageously as Donald Trump, period."[28]

Trump's Opponents

Narcissists brag because they want to appear better than others. They do the same by disparaging others. Trump treated his opponents, and even his allies, quite badly, with ridicule and derision, whether they were Democratic opponents, Republican allies, or foreign leaders. There was "Sleepy Joe (Biden)," "Crazy Bernie (Sanders)," "Cryin' Chuck (Schumer)," "Little Michael (Bloomberg)," "fat Jerry (Nadler)," and "shifty (Adam) Schiff." Those were just the Democrats. There was also "Lyin' Ted (Cruz)," "Little Marco (Rubio)," and "substance-free narcissist" Bobby Jindal "who looks like he has a squirrel sitting on his head."[29] Unsurprisingly, Trump seemed to turn his most vicious vitriol on women, using the names "crooked Hillary (Clinton)," "Pocahontas (Elizabeth Warren)," "crazy little Liz (Cheney)," "that woman from Michigan (Gretchen Whitmore)," and "dumb as a rock Mika

27. Kessler, "Trump Made Misleading Claims."
28. Beschloss, in Timm, "Trump Versus the Truth."
29. Flores, "Donald Trump's Feud."

(Brezinski)." Regarding Republican opponent Carly Fiorina, Trump said, "Look at that face. Would anyone vote for that face?" And when Megyn Kelly pressed Trump about misogynistic, sexist comments he had made in the past, such as calling women "fat pigs, dogs, slobs, and disgusting animals," Trump said of Kelly, "You could see there was blood coming out of her eyes. Blood coming out of her wherever."[30] Similarly, Trump denigrated world leaders Theresa May as "stupid" and Angela Merkel as "a fool." And he variously referred to Kamala Harris as "Nasty Kamala," "nasty woman," and "phony Kamala." And these are just a few examples, but you get the idea.

Trump was and is obsessed by his need to "win," such that his principal goal since he entered politics has always been first to achieve and then maintain his presidency. He spent far more time and energy seeking to overthrow a legitimate election than he ever spent seeking policy. Like all leaders with fragile egos, Trump could never truly meet the needs of the people of his base, because he never truly cared about them. He cared only about himself.

Trump's Base

Initially, Donald Trump's base consisted of the "ordinary people"—the common people who felt disrespected and ignored. Modified more rigorously over time, the demographics of his base are now well-defined. Annual household incomes of supporters are usually below the median (which was just under $60,000 in 2016). His supporters are generally non-college educated. They tend to be rural, white, and are more likely to be men than women. They include rightwing white evangelical Christians, as well as some people of other Christian denominations. Of course, these are generalizations and individual supporters may in fact be quite diverse.

Most importantly, the people of Trump's base are often unemployed or working in unsatisfactory jobs. These are people who had once held the "good" jobs—the jobs in manufacturing, mining, and farming—and they had once felt valued and appreciated. They had been productive and received good wages for their work and fair prices for the products they produced. They handed these good jobs down over generations and were proud to do so.

---

30. Yan, "Donald Trump's 'Blood' Comment."

But the U.S. economy has changed in fundamental ways over the last several decades, making the contributions of many of these workers increasingly obsolete. A combination of technological advance, international trade, climate change, and shifting demand has altered our production methods and moved our economy away from producing one set of goods toward the production of other goods and especially more services. Robotics replaced workers in the auto industry. Relatively abundant and therefore cheap foreign labor replaced U.S. workers in assembly-line production of manufactured goods. Climate change forced us to search for clean energy. And the U.S. demand for services shifted jobs away from the relatively high wage-paying manufacturing sector towards lower wage-paying service occupations. As a result, there is a relative abundance of jobs in service occupations such as healthcare, retail sales, finance, insurance, consulting, intellectual technology, fast food, childcare, education, and others (at least until recently,) The United States has been replaced by other countries as efficient producers of many manufactured goods.

Similarly, changes in the agriculture sector and in coal mining reduced the demand for workers in these industries. Farming has become more concentrated and government benefits accrue more heavily to large and/or corporate farmers. Coal mining extraction has become an expensive way to acquire energy, as well as a dangerous one in terms of black lung disease and environmental harm. Jobs in green energy are expanding at the expense of traditional fossil fuel-based energy.

Along with a loss of jobs in manufacturing, farming, and coal mining came a feeling of lost respect. And it is natural for people who feel disrespected, ignored, and forgotten to crave the attention of a politician who speaks to their issues, promising that they will be listened to, they will be remembered, and they will again be great.

Donald Trump assured his base that as they faced the elite establishment, he would have their backs.

The Elite Establishment

In his acceptance speech for the Republican presidential nomination in July 2016, Donald Trump referenced the elite establishment and used it to explain how the system "is rigged":

> Some of our nation's most powerful special interests ... have rigged
> our political and economic system for their exclusive benefit ...

Big business, elite media and major donors are lining up behind the campaign of my opponent because they know she will keep our rigged system in place.[31]

Trump's opponent was former Secretary of State Hillary Clinton, and she quickly become a target of Trump's attacks. She represented the Washington establishment that upheld the "rigged system" Trump had pledged to take down.

No longer can we rely on those same people, in the media and politics, who will say anything to keep our rigged system in place. Instead, we must choose to believe in America. History is watching us now.[32]

Ironically, Trump would eventually use the same terminology of a "rigged election" to explain his 2020 re-election defeat.

Nevertheless, in the last weeks of the 2016 campaign, Trump's new battle cry was simple:

I will drain the swamp.[33]

The "swamp" referred to Washington, D.C. politicians, government officials, corporate interests, lobbyists, and media. Referring to Clinton, Trump said she "stood with the elites." As it was, Clinton reinforced Trump's accusation with a bad choice of words:

Half of Trump's supporters belong in a "basket of deplorables.[34]

"She went on to explain she was referring to people with "racist, sexist, homophobic, xenophobic, and Islamophobic" views, but this part of her speech fell on deaf ears. By now the base was fundamentally framed as a group of people denigrated by the Clinton, a.k.a. the Washington, D.C. establishment.

Clinton made a bad situation worse when she sought to project empathy for the other half of Trump's supporters who "feel that the government has let them down", but she came off as patronizing.

31. Trump, Jul 21, 2016, "She Will Keep Our Rigged System in Place," in *NPR MPR News,* "Trump's Speech on Clinton."

32. Trump, Jul 21, 2016, "History is Watching Us Now," in *NPR MPR News,* "Trump's Speech on Clinton."

33. Trump, Oct 18, 2016, "I Will Drain the Swamp," in *The American Presidency Project,* "A Video Message from President-Elect Donald J. Trump."

34. Clinton, in Reilly, "Hillary Clinton's 'Basket of Deplorables' Remarks."

Those are people we have to understand and empathize with as well.[35]

While her intent may have been genuine, the damage had been done, and the verbiage stuck. Clinton's use of the word "deplorables" will go down in the history of presidential campaigns.

To be clear, the "Washington establishment" is a real thing, but the notion of "elite" extends beyond Clinton and Washington. For Trump, it came to include "media elites" (e.g., the *New York Times*, the *Washington Post*, MSNBC, and CNN) and the "elites who led us from one financial and foreign policy disaster to another" (referencing former President Barak Obama and Vice President Joe Biden). There were "technology elites" (Amazon and Facebook), academic elites (highly educated urbanites), wealthy liberal elites (Michael Bloomberg and George Soros), and even sports elites (sports station ESPN and the National Football League). Trump used the concept of elites for airing personal grievances against individuals and companies, adding them to his Twitter assaults and linking them to the establishment. He eventually attacked Twitter itself, and ironically, Twitter ultimately barred him from using his Twitter account.

Eventually, Trump reclaimed the notion of elitism for his 2020 campaign. He said in Arizona,

> You know what? I think we're the elites.[36]

He ramped it up in Minnesota as he reminded his supporters of Clinton and the Washington establishment, and he reminded them of the term Clinton had used.

> Why are they elite? I have a much better apartment than they do. I'm smarter than they are. I'm richer than they are. I became president, and they didn't. And I'm representing the greatest, smartest, most loyal, best people on earth—the deplorables.[37]

He amplified it further in South Carolina, saying that he and his voters:

---

35. Clinton, in Reilly, "Hillary Clinton's 'Basket of Deplorables' Remarks."

36. Trump, Aug 21, 2017, "I Think We're The Elites," in Seipel, "Trump Blasts Liberal Elites."

37. Trump, Aug 21, 2017, "Why Are They Elite?" in Seipel, "Trump Blasts Liberal Elites."

are now the elite, the new elite, the super-elite.[38]

And he reminded his supporters in West Virginia,

Just remember that you are the elite.[39]

Trump's Scapegoats

What really riled Trump about the elite establishment was its frequent support for immigrants and people of color. Trump, like other populists, especially blamed "illegals" for the job loss and decline in status of their followers. The populists chose to ignore the real-world forces of changing economics and technology and their role in shifting jobs from one market to another. Immigrants and people of color became Trump's scapegoats, just as they are the scapegoats of populists everywhere.

Immigrants

During his first presidential campaign, Trump pledged to stop illegal immigration and build a border wall that would be funded by Mexico. He charged that Mexicans "are bringing drugs, and bringing crime, and they're rapists."[40] During his presidency, Trump continued, "you wouldn't believe how bad these people are. These aren't people, these are animals."[41] Later in 2018, he targeted immigrants from Central America, especially those travelling in "caravans." He called them "stone cold criminals" and he declared "This is an invasion of our Country [sic] and our Military [sic] is waiting for you!"[42] Another time, Trump questioned the admission of African immigrants from "shithole countries," also asking, "Why do we need more Haitians? . . . They all have AIDS."[43] He regularly disparaged refugee

---

38. Trump, Nov 1, 2018, "The Super-Elite," in Thomsen, "Trump: My supporters Should Be Called the 'Super Elite.'"

39. Trump, Nov 1, 2018, "Just Remember," in *CBS News,* "You Are The Elite."

40. Trump, Jun 16, 2015, "They're Racists," in Gabbatt, "Trump's Tirade."

41. Trump, May 15, 2018, "These are Animals," in Gomez, "Trump Ramps Up Rhetoric."

42. Trump, Nov 26, 2018, "This Is An invasion Of Our Country," in Arce, "Trump's Immigration Tirade."

43. Trump, Jan 11, 2018, "They All Have AIDS." in *The Washington Post,* "'The Haitians all have Aids.'"

populations of Hispanic and Somali Americans living in U.S. communities, and often retweeted hateful and deceitful messages about these and other immigrants. He promised white communities that refugees would not be allowed to settle in locations where they were not wanted.

Trump's immigration policy was draconian, the product of his own viciousness and that of senior adviser, Stephen Miller. Trump drastically cut the U.S. refugee program, bringing the number of refugees admitted into the United States to the lowest level since the program began in 1948. He dismantled the immigration infrastructure to the point where we haven't yet fully regained it. He sought to end the Temporary Protected Status (TPS) of immigrants who had escaped crises in their home countries, as well as the Deferred Action for Childhood Arrivals (DACA) program that protected young people brought to the United States illegally as children. Most importantly, he eliminated the practice he derided as "catch and release," which permitted most immigrants crossing the southern border illegally to file asylum requests and await adjudication on their own within the United States. Typically, these asylum seekers were rather quickly detained by border agents once they crossed the border, or they immediately turned themselves in to the authorities. They were not criminals, and they had no alternative means of entering the country during this period under Trump. To suggest otherwise means to ignore the realities of our broken immigration system.

Just as the phrase, "catch and release," was meant to denigrate immigrants by comparing them to animals, Trump used the derogatory phrase "chain migration" to refer to the families of immigrants who subsequently sought to immigrate to the United States. Family immigration has always been the foundation of the U.S. immigration system and is based on both humanitarian concerns and the fact it lends greater stability to families, communities, and the entire immigration system. In fact, Trump's wife, Melania, brought her parents to the United States via so called "chain migration." While our national immigration system remains woefully inadequate, family immigration remains an important part of it. Pope Francis believes this is as it should be:

> Don't we all want a better, more decent and prosperous life to share with our loved ones?[44]

---

44. Pope Francis, in *Universe of Faith*, "Pope Francis' Quotes."

Trump replaced the "catch and release" policy with a an even more insidious policy of "zero tolerance," with which he detained immigrant adults in detention centers while they awaited the outcome of their asylum claims. U.S. law, however, places restrictions on the detention of children, forcing authorities to take them from their parents and hold them separately from their families. As a result, little children were photographed as they were ripped from their mothers' arms, placed in overcrowded cages, and cared for by older children rather than adults. This was perhaps the singular most unpopular policy of the Trump Administration, moving the hearts of many Americans (who had never protested before) to rally against the mistreatment of these children. To this day, many of these children have not been reunited with their families because the government failed to keep adequate track of their locations and those of their parents.

Unbelievably, U.S. immigration policy only got worse from there. Trump established what was misleadingly called the "Migrant Protection Protocols," which, rather than being protective, subjected asylum-seekers to danger as they were forced to await their court dates in Mexico. Alternatively called the "Remain in Mexico policy," this practice forced immigrants to leave the United States after filing asylum claims and await their adjudication in crowded, squalid, and dangerous camps along the Mexican side of the border for months and even years. Those who felt they could not wait any longer sometimes sought to enter the United States illegally. This is when we witnessed the scenes of women and children being teargassed and mistreated by border agents. And, in the same way that a photo of a boy who had washed up onto the shores of the Mediterranean had stolen the hearts of many across the world, a photo of a little girl and her father who had washed up onto the shores of the Rio Grande once again broke those very same hearts.

Trump later took advantage of the COVID-19 pandemic as an excuse to enforce Title 42 under the Public Health Service Act to further limit immigration, claiming that immigrants posed a risk of spreading the virus. Of course, COVID-19 cases were higher in the United States than in Mexico, and an alternative would have been to test and quarantine immigrants until they could safely enter the country.

Trump's disgraceful border policies stemmed from his outrageous attitudes and sick desires for human butchery. Former Department of Homeland Security Chief of Staff Miles Taylor claimed that Trump told administration officials he wanted to "shoot" migrants at the southern border.

He added that Trump would concoct "sickening" schemes "to pierce the flesh" of migrants, to "maim" them, and despite the Holocaust images they elicited, he wanted to gas them.[45] Furthermore, it was reported that Trump suggested fortifying a border wall with a water-filled trench (a moat), which would be stocked with snakes or alligators.[46]

Immigrants bring important economic benefits to the United States and other similarly developed countries. As workers, they enable businesses to prosper and expand. They also take the undesirable jobs unfilled by current residents. As consumers, their demand for goods and services encourages expanded production of these products and therefore results in job creation. As entrepreneurs, immigrants enhance the vitality of local business districts. As taxpayers, they fund any services they and their children receive; and as young workers, they bulk up a social security system increasingly threatened by an aging population. Aside from economic benefits, immigrants enhance the diversity of our communities, help fill our schools and churches, and revitalize our neighborhoods. Crime rates fall in the communities where immigrants settle, and immigrants from other countries bring to us and our children a broader vision and worldview. The pope summarizes the benefits of diversity as follows:

> The arrival of those who are different, coming from other ways of life and cultures, can be a gift . . . For the communities and societies to which they come, migrants bring an opportunity for enrichment and the integral human development of all.[47]

People of Color

Even before Trump ran for the presidency, his family was long involved with redlining and other racist practices in their real estate business activities.[48] As early as 2011, Trump was espousing his "birther theories" that questioned the American birth of former President Barak Obama. And as we'll note later in the book, it was over ten years earlier that Trump paid for TV ads advocating for the death penalty after five Black and Hispanic

---

45. Taylor, et al., "President Wanted to 'Maim' Migrants."
46. Tarlo, "Trump Wanted U.S. Forces Equipped With Bayonets."
47. Pope Francis, *Fratelli Tutti*, 133
48. Redlining is the practice of denying mortgages in minority neighborhoods.

boys were convicted (and later exonerated) of raping a woman in Central Park.

Trump's racism ramped up as the 2016 election approached and it continued throughout his presidency and post-presidency. Along with immigrants, people of color became scapegoats amidst Trump's culture wars. He stoked the fears of white people as he lied about violence, and he charged the elite with supporting reverse discrimination. He took his rallies to white suburbs, telling his suburban followers that he would prevent the construction of low-cost multifamily dwellings in their communities. It was evident that by "low-cost" housing he meant "Black housing," and by "Black housing" he meant "crime infested housing." He led his white followers to fear Black Lives Matter and oppose "defunding the police," which never actually meant defunding the police. As a result, white families demanded expanded police protection. They showed up at City Hall discussions of police protection, zoning laws, and multifamily housing; and they badgered their school boards to oppose desegregation if it meant children of color would join their own children in the classroom. Far better to homeschool or enroll their children in private schools, while supporting a president who would shift massive amounts of funding away from public schools to private ones in the form of vouchers.

Unfortunately, the assault on our schools has gone far beyond this, and far beyond Donald Trump. By 2021 and 2022, rightwing Republicans were demanding that "woke" education be abolished and "critical race theory" be forbidden. By woke education, they were referring to an accurate portrayal of U.S. history, including the genocide against Native Americans and the slave trade against Africans and African Americans. They said their concern was protecting the feelings of white children, for whom they wanted no sense of guilt. This is understandable as far as it goes, but it goes entirely too far when teachers are barred from teaching certain subjects and saying certain words, and school libraries are barred from carrying certain books. Students have the right to know an accurate depiction of history.

Rightwing conservatives never did understand the meaning of critical race theory, which is a topic addressed in law schools and goes to the structural underpinnings of our society and its institutions that contribute to racism and inequity for people of color. No public grade school has ever taught critical race theory, yet swarms of people began bombarding school board meetings across the country, demanding that critical race theory not be taught. Like healthcare providers administering COVID-19 vaccinations and neutral poll workers doing their patriotic duty, teachers and school board members became the targets of demonstrators, stalkers, and even those who would harm them and their children for carrying out proper teaching responsibilities.

As the 2022 midterm elections approached, Donald Trump's racist rhetoric increased, along with that of other populist politicians. In one rambling rant on his Truth Social platform, Trump warned that American Jews need to "get their act together" before "it is too late!"[49] This suggestion that American Jews were disloyal to Trump played into the antisemitic trope that U.S. Jews have dual loyalties to the United States and to Israel. Trump added that "No President has done more for Israel than I have," and he rather oddly augmented his post to say it was somewhat surprising that "our wonderful Evangelicals are far more appreciative of this than the people of the Jewish faith, especially those living in the U.S."[50]

This wasn't the first time Trump complained about American Jews, who have traditionally aligned themselves with the Democratic party on domestic policies. In an interview with an Orthodox Jewish magazine, he said, "Jewish people who live in the United States don't love Israel enough. Does that make sense to you?"[51] He added that it seemed "strange" to him that he didn't have more Jewish support. And, at a Hanukkah event at the White House in 2018, Trump referred to Israel as "your country" while speaking to American Jews,[52] and in 2019, he said that if "any Jewish people who vote for a Democrat, I think it shows either a total lack of knowledge or great disloyalty."[53]

By February 2022, Trump returned to racism against Asians—he had stopped talking about the "Kung flu" and "Chinese virus," likely because he was no longer talking about COVID-19—and he began racist name-calling of Elaine Chao, his Taiwanese-born former secretary of transportation and the wife of Senate Minority Leader Mitch McConnell. He called her "Coco Chow" in an angry statement that is typical of his proclivity for demeaning

49. Trump, Oct 15, 2022, "Get Their Act Together," in *The Washington Post*, "The Haitians All Have AIDS."

50. Trump, Oct 16, 2022, "No President Has Done More," in Seipel, "Trump Again Claims."

51. Trump, June 17, 2021, "Jewish People," in Fink, "Jewish People."

52. Trump, Jan 27, 2023, "Any Jewish People Who Vote For A Democrat," in D'Abrosca, "Trump Blasts Jews."

53. Trump, Jan 20, 2017, "A Total Lack Of Knowledge Or Great Disloyalty," in Vazquez and Acosta, "Jewish Leaders Outraged."

name-calling, particularly towards women. One year later, he called her "Coco Chow" again, while trying to connect Chao and Mitch McConnell to classified documents found in President Biden's office in Washington, D.C. Trump said, "Does Coco Chow have anything to do with Joe Biden's Classified Documents being sent and stored in Chinatown? Her husband, the Old Broken Crow, is VERY close to Biden the Democrats, and of course, China."[54]

Some would argue that Trump's racism motivated the racism of others in his party, but it is more likely that it legitimized what many of them had wanted all along. After all, one doesn't become a racist overnight. However, racism suddenly became "acceptable," and Republican politicians were not chided by their fellow Republicans for their racist language.

We can't help but recognize that our policies and institutions are premised on contempt for the poor, the immigrant, and the person of color. We will address these scapegoats and populism's "discarded people" more broadly in Chapter 5–6.

TRUMP'S NATIONALISM

As we've noted, populism is even more perilous when coupled with nationalism. While the form of nationalism can vary across countries, it is a frequent partner to populism. And just as with populism, Trump defined nationalism with a slogan:

America First.

While Donald Trump's inaugural address described his populist view of America, it also described his vision of America vis à vis the rest of the world. Trump aligned the populism of "Make America Great Again" with the nationalism of "America First."

> From this day forward, a new vision will govern our land. From this day forward, it's going to be only America first, America first. Every decision on trade, on taxes, on immigration, on foreign affairs will be made to benefit American workers and American families..[55]

---

54. Trump, Jan 27, 2023, "Coco Chow," in Paybarah, "Does Coco Chow Have Anything To Do With Joe Biden's Classified Documents?"

55. Trump, Jan 20, 2017, "From This Day Forward," in "The Full Text of Donald Trump's Inauguration Address," *The Guardian*.

Perhaps this sounds appealing. Perhaps it sounds proper. But as suggested earlier, it is based on the premise that the world is a "zero-sum game." In other words, nationalistic populists believe there is only so much "good" in the world, whether this "good" refers to productive resources, consumer products, or in Trump's case, money and wealth. American populists believe that more money and wealth for other countries means less money and wealth for America.[56]

We know this isn't true, and caring solely for oneself, whether individual or country, is never a route to greatness. Over the course of Trump's presidency, he assailed U.S. allies and seemingly backed our adversaries. The European Union became "our number one enemy" and Canada became "an adversary." Trump imposed trade restrictions to harm other countries, but he ended up harming his own. He pulled the United States out of the North American Free Trade Agreement (NAFTA) and ceased to participate in the planning for the Trans-Pacific Partnership (TPP). Both of these decisions were detrimental to U.S. producers and workers. Trump removed the United States from the Paris Climate Accord (thereby worsening climate change), the World Health Organization (during a pandemic), and the Iranian nuclear agreement (thereby enabling Iran to break the terms of the agreement and advance its uranium). Trump slashed U.S. foreign aid, despite the reality that foreign aid is essential for humanitarian reasons and is vital to global stability. And he abruptly pulled the United States out of Syria, causing the death of multitudes of Syrians, Kurds, and others. Trump did all of these, purportedly to benefit the United States. In all cases, he harmed our nation instead.

As indicated earlier in the book, nationalism can take the form of white Christian nationalism, which attempts to connect Christianity with American civic life. Christian nationalists often equate God and country as they preach about how God has favored the United States as a Christian state, and oddly enough, they see Donald Trump as a leader chosen by God. I say this is odd, because for most of us, the behavior and rhetoric of

---

56. Trump's view of a "zero sum game" may trace back to his business dealings. Accountants use balance sheets to keep track of money coming in and going out, but financial accounting sheets don't tell the full story of the mutual benefits of trade, for example. Similarly, Trump was wrongly convinced that U.S. tariffs are paid by foreign exporters and not U.S. importers; and he failed to properly understand how European counties financially support NATO. At one point Trump was publicly corrected by Prime Minister Justin Trudeau when he erroneously referenced a U.S. trade deficit with Canada. Trump's economic advisers were largely non-economists who seemed unwilling or unable to correct Trump's misconceptions.

Trump does not seem divinely inspired. Christian nationalists focus on his policies, which often support traditional values of white American families. It is nevertheless somewhat of a paradox that Christian nationalists favor Trump, who is not religious and doesn't regularly attend church, over President Biden, who is a devout Catholic who regularly attends Mass.

Finally, we observe that nationalistic populists, whether they are white Christian nationalists or not, can very well tend towards authoritarianism.

TRUMP'S AUTHORITARIANISM

We've noted that Trump was attracted to military ceremonies. He was also attracted to authoritarian leaders, seeking the attention of the world's greatest bullies. He praised Philippine dictator, Rodrigo Duterte, and invited him to visit the United States. At the time, Duterte's violent crackdown on drugs had already left over 7,000 of his countrymen dead. Referring to China's Xi Jinping, Trump said, "He is a good man. He is a very good man and I got to know him very well."[57] He praised North Korea's Kim Jong-Un, and he fawned over Russia's Vladimir Putin. Referring to Egypt's oppressive military dictator, Trump said,

> President al-Sisi has been somebody that's been very close to me from the first time I met him . . . we are very much behind President al-Sisi . . . And I just want to say to you, Mr. President [al-Sisi], that you have a great friend and ally in the United States and in me.[58]

Trump's authoritarian nature was increasingly revealed throughout his tenure as president. We watched as he broke down American institutions, one by one, and destroyed our democracy bit by bit. He disparaged the media, rendering it untrustworthy in the minds of his supporters. He used Fox News as a megaphone to disseminate his views rather than news. He restricted freedom of speech by utilizing federal troops against peaceful demonstrators. He opposed Black Lives Matter and ANTIFA,[59] while supporting neo-Nazis and white supremacists. He politicized the Justice

57. Trump, May 2, 2017, "He Is A Good Man," in Buckley, "A Spring Thaw?"

58. Trump, Apr 3, 2017, "President al-Sisi," in U.S. Embassy in Egypt, "President al-Sisi Has Been Somebody That's Been Very Close To Me."

59. The term "ANTIFA" is frequently used by Trump and other rightwing politicians as if to describe a violent organization. It is not an organization, but rather a loose compilation of anti-fascist protesters.

Department, the Internal Revenue Service, the Department of Defense, Homeland Security, the Census Bureau, and even the Post Office. All these efforts were designed to maintain Trump's power and assure his reelection. Even the coronavirus pandemic was politicized, to the point where one could almost identify Democrats and Republicans merely by whether or not they wore masks.

As he did in the 2016 election season, Trump insisted amid the 2020 campaigns that the election would be rigged. He made it clear to his followers that if he were to lose the reelection, it was proof that the election was falsified. When he lost his reelection, he devoted all his energy to overturning the results. We learned early on that he and his allies had badgered election officials to change the outcome of the vote. They invented odd conspiracy theories involving a dead Venezuelan leader and fraudulent voting machines. The established fake slates of electors who were to cast their states' ballots for Trump instead of the real winner. Trump appointed an attorney general and a secretary of defense for the explicit purpose of helping to ensure he remained in office.

Trump prepared for an insurrection. He called on the Proud Boys, a white supremacist militant group, to "stand down and stand by."[60] He called on his supporters to come to the Capitol on January 6th, stating "Be there, will be wild!"[61] And on that fateful day, Trump whipped his supporters into a frenzy with a rally, telling them to walk to the capitol even as other insurrectionists were already there and preparing for assault. The January 6, 2021, insurrection will go down in history as a violent assault on our nation and the first time in centuries that a peaceful transfer of power from one U.S. president to another did not occur. Trump himself will go down in history as the only disgraced, twice impeached, and later indicted and arrested president who refused to accept his reelection defeat. Our nation's capital truly became one of American carnage.

Trump spent his remaining days in office charging election fraud and hindering the transition of President-elect Joe Biden. It didn't matter that there was a surging pandemic. It didn't matter that Russia had seriously breached America's computer infrastructure. It didn't matter that the transition period itself is notoriously susceptible to foreign misdeeds.

60. Trump, Sep 29, 2020, "Stand Back and Stand By," in McCarthy, "Stand Back and Stand By."

61. Trump, Jan 19, 2020, "Be There, Will Be Wild!" in Barry and Frenkel, "Be There. Will Be Wild!"

The one thing that mattered was the president's ego. The forgotten people of the base became forgotten once again; and the eleven weeks from the election to Biden's inauguration left the nation to spin on its own.

How did America get here?

To this day, Trump's supporters believe the election was stolen, leaving America at a crossroads. How will the country cope with a post-election electorate that is split in half—with one side supporting Trump and the other side Biden? How do Americans contend with each other when they carry entirely different worldviews, often reinforced by entirely different news sources and completely different "sets of facts"? How do we unite as a country when one of our two major parties is now associated with white supremacism, white militancy, and the disenfranchisement of people of color? And how do we survive as a democracy when this same political party is seeking to grant its state legislatures the right to reject election results if their preferred candidate loses?

American society is at a crossroads, but it is not alone. Much of Europe and even countries in Africa, Asia, and Latin America are grappling with the tensions of populism, nationalism, and authoritarianism in their midst. We will address the role of the various ideologies in countries across the world in Chapter 4.

QUESTIONS FOR DISCUSSION

1. What are our shared values, as people of faith and no faith, as Democrats and Republicans, as populists and progressives, and as people of this nation? Do we, in fact, have any shared values?

2. How do our values reflect our political choices?

3. Who among the scapegoats are our sisters and brothers? Be specific.

4. Were you offended about some of the comments about Donald Trump? If so, why is this?

5. Do you believe Donald Trump is a white supremacist? If not, why not?

Chapter 4

Global Trumpism
Populism, Nationalism, and Authoritarianism

FIRST, I ENCOURAGE YOU to get a map of Europe, as well as a map of the world. These will help you understand the geography of Europe and the developing world, along with regional immigration routes.

As we will see, immigration plays and has played a leading role in the development and ramifications of populism throughout the world and not just in the United States.

IMMIGRATION

The Arab Spring

The Arab Spring was a democracy movement that occurred throughout many of the Arab countries in the Middle East and North Africa. The movement began in Tunisia in 2010, and then spread to Libya, Egypt, Yemen, Syria, and Bahrain with major protests and civil wars that rose up against dictators and oppressive governments that were tyrannizing their citizens. Smaller scale protests occurred in Lebanon, Jordan, Sudan, Palestine, Saudi Arabia, Western Sahara, and several other countries. The Arab Spring met with varying degrees of success, and in many cases, the outcome was prolonged civil war, failure to remove dictators, and even greater tyranny than before. Let's focus for a moment on Syria, which provides a good example of the violence that ensued after the failed efforts of the country's Arab Spring.

Protests broke out in Syria in March 2011, with activists calling for the resignation of President Bashar al-Assad. These protests spread throughout the country, and the Assad regime responded with brutal crackdowns. Violence escalated as funding and armaments arrived from other countries that began using Syria as a proxy location for their own wars, and a full-blown civil war with the addition of regional players ensued. Iran and Russia were the principal supporters of al-Assad, who attacked his own population with chemical weapons, bombs, and explosives. The ones who suffered most were the civilians, including the multitudes of children and their families holed up in their basements, terrorized and waiting for the nonstop bombing to end. The outcome was a massive refugee crisis involving millions.

European Immigration

Many other countries experienced a similarly failed Arab Spring and were devastated by the subsequent violence and poverty. Suddenly, immigration from Syria to Europe evolved into a mass migration of desperate people from many parts of the world, including the Asian countries of India, Philippines, Myanmar, and Iraq, and multiple African countries. Juxtaposed on all of this are the millions of internally displaced and refugee populations fleeing their homes in Afghanistan. Immigrants from some countries entered Europe directly, while others gathered in the northern African countries on their way to Europe. And then there was Ukraine.

The War in Ukraine

On February 21, 2022, Russian President Vladimir Putin invaded Ukraine. U.S. President Biden responded with the words,

> Who in the Lord's name does Putin think gives him the right? . . .
> This is a flagrant violation of international law, and it demands a
> firm response from the international community.[1]

And with these words, the world changed, and the future suddenly became unknown.

While it is difficult to define the ideology of Vladmir Putin other than as "Putinism," he can clearly be classified as an authoritarian. And Russia's

1. Biden, "Remarks by President Biden."

influence is widespread. The Russian Imperial Movement, for example, is an ultranationalist group that is believed to be training neo-Nazi militants in Western Europe and supporting election interference in the United States. The group has active links to white supremacists in the United States. Perhaps most unsettling is the number of far-right U.S. Republicans and white supremacists who now openly admire Vladmir Putin.

The United Nations anticipates five to seven million Ukrainian refugees fleeing into Europe, the United States, and elsewhere. While there are parallels with the Arab Spring, this mass immigration is unique insofar as Ukrainian refugees are white, European, and largely Christian. The ramifications are already evident. The United States is accepting Ukrainian immigrants ahead of immigrants from the Americas who have already been waiting far too long. And European countries that rejected non-white immigrants are welcoming Ukrainian refugees with open arms. The difference in reaction can be due to multiple factors, but clearly one is a greater willingness of white people to welcome white people.

U.S. Immigration

In addition to Ukrainian refugees, similar large-scale immigration is taking place in the United States as people flee conflict-ridden countries around the world. These include people escaping from African countries including Liberia, Eritrea, and Somalia; and from the Asian countries just mentioned. Also prominent among immigrants to the United States are the asylum-seekers approaching the southern U.S. border from Mexico, Haiti, Venezuela, and Cuba, as well as from the Northern Triangle countries of Central America (El Salvador, Guatemala, and Honduras).

Most recently, tens of thousands of people lost their lives and their homes in massive earthquakes in Turkey and Syria in February 2023. While the ramifications are yet unknown, they will undoubtedly include vast displacement and global immigration.

Other Causes of Immigration

Drug Gangs

In the Northern Triangle countries and in Haiti, violent gangs and drug dealers continue to terrorize much of the population, and people are killed for witnessing crimes, resisting paying bribes, failing to pay protection money, and refusing to join the gangs. The level of violence is unimaginable to most of us in the United States, and it is hard to imagine it being sufficient to cause people to leave their homes. Many victims have already lost family members, however, and are in no mood to continue risking their lives and the lives of their remaining family.

Climate Change

Climate change is another characteristic of our world today that is motivating increased conflict and greater migration. Due to our warming planet, populations are experiencing more severe and frequent famines, storms, fires, home loss, crop loss, and damaged livelihoods. Conflict ensues as resources become scarcer. For example, farmers and herders in parts of Africa had previously had amiable and symbiotic relationships. The animals of herders left deposits of fertilizer on the land of farmers, who in turn allowed the herders to graze their livestock on the farmland. Now, many of these people are in direct conflict over increasingly limited land, water, and other resources. And, in addition to the violent gang activity just addressed, immigrants to the United States from the Northern Triangle in Central America are fleeing the severe storms associated with climate change.

Poverty and Racism

Appalling poverty also leads to immigration. Along with poverty comes unspeakable hardship (such as dangerous and exhausting labor by entire families) and deprivation (insufficient food, medicine, and even housing). Poverty forces families to flee just as desperately as others flee violence.

RIGHTWING IDEOLOGY

While immigration may have been a trigger for rightwing ideologies, white supremacy and neo-Naziism didn't just spring up suddenly in reaction to immigration. These ideologies had been ready and waiting for the right moment. The right moment had come, and the anti-Semitics, anti-Islamists, and white supremacists came out into the open across the world. And while immigration has been a catalyst for rightwing ideology, there are also other factors at play, including social media.

Social media permits the spewing of hate speech and provides a platform for conspiracy theorists to circulate racist fantasies and lies. It provides small groups of people an opportunity to amplify their messages, which when tweeted and retweeted, become outsized voices that belie their initial presence. Social media also provides susceptible "lone wolfs" with schemes and methods for their violent behavior and the ideologies that back them up.

Some observers refer to the "gamification" of terrorism, meaning the use of the Internet to "compete" over death tolls from violent acts. Some purveyors of violence go so far as to videotape and flaunt their violent attacks as if they were addictive games. Meanwhile, gun rights activists keep assault weapons within easy reach of terrorists and conspirators, and as we noted in Chapter 2, campaign ads by political figures now include guns and violent images. Most recently, Trump posted a photo of himself swinging a baseball bat next to a photo of Manhattan District Attorney Alvin Bragg's head, Trump's prosecutor. Bragg has since received multiple death threats.

Unfortunately, those fleeing their homes due to violence, poverty, and climate disasters are met with unimaginable contempt by a far more privileged population on the right. We see this in their words and actions as their ideologies wind their way through Europe and the rest of the world, just as they tunnel their way through the United States. These ideologies are professed by politicians, sometimes at the highest level of leadership. They are reflected in people's movements, and they are displayed with violence. Let's consider a snapshot of the rightwing ideologies as they spread through Europe and the developing world.

WESTERN EUROPE

While Western European countries vary considerably in their place on the left/right spectrum, there is nevertheless a rightwing movement among them. Populism is rising. Nationalism takes the form of opposition to the European Union (and the United Nations, NATO, etc.), in the same sense that U.S. nationalism takes the form of opposition to the rest of the world. Anti-immigrant fervor coincides with mixed feelings on the Ukrainian conflict. Populist parties include Germany's Alternative for Germany, France's National Rally, Spain's Vox, Greece's Golden Dawn, and Italy's Brothers of Italy and the League. Of course, there are many other populist social movements that do not have party affiliations.

Germany

Germany generously welcomed immigrants following the failed Arab Spring, due to the strong leadership of Angela Merkel. Unfortunately, this triggered the rapid spread of anti-immigrant white-supremacist populist movements in the country. The Alternative for Germany (AfD) rose in popularity, and in 2017, it became the first far-right party to win seats in Germany's parliament in sixty years. Rightwing politician Björn Höcke said unkindly that Germany needs a "strong broom" to "clear the pigsty [of immigrants]" who should be met with "well-tempered cruelty."[2] Höcke also criticized Germany's efforts to "atone" for the Holocaust and he openly questions whether Hitler was "entirely evil."[3]

Far-right violent crimes have increased dramatically in Germany in the last few years, which experts link to the rise of the AfG. In 2019, a Jewish synagogue in Germany was attacked by a white supremacist, who killed two people and would have massacred dozens more if his weapons hadn't malfunctioned. Early in the following year, nine people of immigrant backgrounds were fatally shot, presumably by rightwing militants. And in mid-2020, as if to forewarn Americans of the January 6 insurrection, far right protesters in Germany broke through fences and reached the stairs to Berlin's Reichstag (parliament) in what was labeled an "intolerable attack on the heart of democracy."[4]

2. Jordans, "Far Right."
3. Verbeek and Davis, "Berlin Protests."
4. Mahmood and Stern, "Germany Arrests."

Most significantly, in the final days of 2022, German officials arrested dozens of members and supporters of a rightwing militant organization on suspicion of plotting to overthrow the government and replace it with its own order. According to a government statement,

> The accused are united by a deep rejection of state institutions and the free democratic basic order . . . which over time has led to their decision to participate in their violent elimination and to engage in concrete preparatory actions for this purpose.[5]

The government added that there was Russian involvement in plotting the overthrow.

The AfG party has infiltrated all levels of government and is no longer on the sidelines. As in the United States, far-right politicians are making their way into German state and local legislatures in numbers often exceeding those at the federal levels and with more extremist ideology. Antisemitism is becoming more and more visible and seemingly more acceptable. For example, antisemitic spray-painted graffiti was found at the site that once housed the Nazis' largest death camp in Auschwitz. The graffiti included slogans denying that the Holocaust occurred. Because of their historical association with the Holocaust, the words and actions of German rightwing hate groups are particularly alarming.

France

There are multiple far-right players within France's politics today. The "yellow vest movement" consists of protesters (wearing yellow vests, of course) who oppose carbon taxes, coronavirus restrictions, and other "restrictions" on their liberty. While this movement is clearly populist, it is not aligned with any rightwing political parties. However, along with other activist movements that are more rightwing, the yellow vest movement has held multiple rallies and attracted hundreds of thousands of protesters. Another group is Generation Identity, which is a militant youth movement that espouses neo-Nazi views. Additionally, Marine le Pen is a well-known far-right populist who heads the rightwing National Rally.

Paris is home to large numbers of immigrants who are living in tents and shacks. The greater Paris region alone accounts for 44% of homeless people in Francs, and shelter conditions here are more precarious than

5. Brito, et al., "The Accused are United."

elsewhere in the country. Thirty-eight percent of the homeless are women, and the majority of the homeless live alone. Over half of homeless persons (55 percent) were born outside France. Seemingly without concern for their wellbeing, they are regularly uprooted and cleared out by police. It is hard to be an immigrant in a country that is becoming increasingly anti-immigrant.

Scandinavia

One might think the Scandinavian countries of Denmark, Sweden, Norway, Finland, and Iceland would be exempt from far-right extremism, because their strong safety nets and social programs give the appearance of a well-cared for population guaranteed by the government. It is quite the opposite, however, and immigrants are often treated quite badly. The neo-Nazi Nordic Resistance Movement is a terrorist organization that operates in Norway, Sweden, Denmark, and Iceland, though it is banned in Finland. In Sweden, the Sweden Democrats party is openly xenophobic and neo-Nazi protesters there were recently heard chanting, "we will not let in scum [immigrants]." In Denmark, the ruling leftwing Social Democrat Party has shifted its stance on immigration to resemble that of far-right parties. Denmark has also become the first European country to revoke the residency permits of some Syrian refugees, especially single women, despite continued unsafe conditions in Syria. The Danish prime minister recently reiterated her vision for Denmark as having "zero-asylum seekers." Finally, in Norway, many ethnic Norwegians take pride in their cherished white Nordic heritage and oppose its dilution by immigration. Islamophobia was revealed when a heavily armed gunman stormed into a mosque in 2019, intent on killing Muslims, but was tackled and stopped by worshippers. Worse, Norwegians will never forget the day in 2011 when Anders Breivik killed 77 people in a bombing attack on Oslo (a few blocks from where my daughter was working) and a Norwegian youth camping trip.

The Mediterranean Countries

As you look at the map of Europe, you see that the countries of Cyprus, Greece, Spain, and Italy (among others) border the Mediterranean Sea and are in relative proximity to the northern African countries of Morocco, Algeria, Tunisia, Libya, and Egypt. As such, northern Africa is often a drop-off point for people escaping violence and poverty throughout Africa and elsewhere in the region and seeking immigration into Europe by crossing the Mediterranean Sea. Often departing in flimsy and overcrowded boats arranged by smugglers, thousands of Africans and others have drowned. The true number of deaths in unknown, as the Mediterranean has become a graveyard for desperate migrants.

Among the Mediterranean countries mentioned, Cyprus receives a relatively large number of immigrants per population. Its asylum process is slow, and people feel like prisoners in the detention camps where they are held. In Spain, thousands of immigrants swim from the shores of Morocco, with many of them arriving exhausted and shivering (and others washing up dead.) Spain's anti-immigrant populist Vox party sends many of the surviving immigrants directly back to Morocco. Greece's far-right neo-Nazi Golden Dawn party has risen to become the country's third-largest party. The party was recently charged by the International Criminal Court as a criminal organization for its treatment of immigrants. Founded as a neo-Nazi group in 1982, it is seen as a model for many extreme-right groups worldwide.

Lastly, Giorgia Meloni was recently elected as Italy's first female prime minister, and she leads the country's most far-right government since World War II. As a populist and nationalist, she has had allies in France's Marine Le Pen and the Spanish Vox party. Meloni is the leader of the hard-right Brothers of Italy, which descended from Italy's earlier experience with fascism. Her ruling coalition includes Silvio Berlusconi of the Forza Italia party, who is a friend of Vladimir Putin and blames Ukraine for the war. Maloni's other coalition partner is Matteo Salvini, the leader of the anti-migrant League and a Putin supporter. The League is not only anti-immigrant, but also vehemently anti-Muslim, and has rallied for a pro-white culture in the European Union. One member of the League summed up its populist attitude: "This Europe . . . of bureaucrats, do-gooders, bankers, boats of migrants [must be changed]."

Prime Minister Meloni has a long history of making incendiary speeches against the European Union. She once considered leaving the euro zone, and she was previously aligned with the rightwing leader of Hungary, who we will consider in a moment. She is strongly anti-immigrant and has proposed a naval blockade to stop immigrants coming from Africa. She complains that they are *replacing* native Italians.

The United Kingdom

As noted, populism in Western Europe is associated with the region's own versions of nationalism. These include movements in some countries to separate from the European Union, with Brexit being the most prominent. The population of Britain voted to "exit Britain" from the European Union in what was eventually a very messy and chaotic break under a very messy and chaotic Prime Minister Boris Johnson (more recently replaced by another conservative leader). Meanwhile, the police department in London has been charged with racist and discriminatory practices, including the vast overrepresentation of Black people stopped and searched in their vehicles. Here we see a parallel between the systemic racism within British and American police departments. The mayor of London recently announced major efforts to reform, as have mayors of similar American cities.

EASTERN EUROPE

While populist movements and parties have spread across Europe, the most prominent of the populist leaders are in Eastern Europe. These include Prime Minister Viktor Orbán of Hungary, President Alexander Lukashenko of Belarus, President Andrzej Duda of Poland, and until recently, Prime Minister Janez Janša of Slovenia (who made headlines by congratulating Donald Trump on his 2020 "victory" against Biden). We will consider these leaders and a few other examples of eastern European populism.

Hungary

Prime Minister Viktor Orbán is strongly anti-immigrant and authoritarian, and he is a white Christian nationalistic. In response to what he recently decried as a "flood" of migrants being "forced" upon his country, he proclaimed he wants to prevent his Hungary from becoming a mix-raced country. He is charged by Europe's leading human rights agency, the Council of Europe, with caging, starving, and denying legal representation for refugees amassed along Hungary's border with Serbia. Taking care of them wasn't even a consideration, according to a document released by the Hungarian government that states Hungarian authorities have no "obligation to provide *catering* after the final closure of the asylum procedure."[6] The word

6. Santora and Novak, "Hungary's Migrant Abuse."

"catering" is italicized to emphasize the contempt that underlies a refusal to feed those denied asylum. Nationalism in Hungary takes the form of opposition to the European Union and the United Nations, which are viewed as remote elites that have no right to govern Hungary. Orbán expresses his authoritarian nature by controlling the media and the courts and by suppressing protests and dissent. In a nod to similar Trumpian policies, some people believe that Hungary seeks to eliminate immigrants by making their conditions intolerable.

CPAC held its convention in Hungary for the second time in 2022. CPAC is the American Conservative Political Action Conference. During his opening address, Orbán called Hungary "the bastion of conservative Christian values in Europe."[7] Orbán has led the country for a dozen years, but like Vladmir Putin, is receiving newfound attention from the American right. This began with words of approval by Donald Trump, and more recently by former rightwing Fox celebrity Tucker Carlson and various rightwing politicians. Orbán's portrayal as a cult figure is not unlike that of Trump. And he has a message to America. From the CPAP stage, he urged U.S. conservatives to defeat "the dominance of progressive liberals in public life," as he says he has done in Hungary. "We must take the institutions back in Washington and Brussels. We must find allies in one another . . ."[8]

It is interesting to note that Pope Francis recently visited Orbán, with the goal of reforming the prime minister's intolerance of Jews, Muslims, and other immigrants. He told him, "the cross . . . raises and extends its arms toward everyone."[9] There is no indication that Orbán has reformed his ways.

Belarus

Belarus is Ukraine's neighbor to the north, and it borders Russia on its eastern side. Belarus is an authoritarian state in which its president, Aleksandr Lukashenka, firmly controls the military and security forces. Elections are falsified and civil liberties are restricted. Lukashenka was reelected in 2020 in what was considered a fraudulent election, resulting in a massive pro-democracy protest movement. Since then, Belarus forces have cracked down severely. Security forces have violently assaulted and arbitrarily detained

7. Spike, "Hungary to Host Conservative Conference."
8. Garamvolgyi, "Viktor Orbán Tells CPAC."
9. Reese, "Pope Calls on World."

journalists and ordinary citizens who challenge the regime, whether by means of protesting, reporting on events, or posting opinions online. The judiciary and other institutions lack independence and provide no check on Lukashenka's power.

One recent event of note occurred when Belarusian authorities forced a flight traveling from Greece to Lithuania to make an emergency landing in Belarus capital of Minsk to arrest exiled blogger and opposition activist Raman Pratasevich. In response, the European Union banned Belarusian airlines from entering its airspace and from accessing its airports. Belarusian authorities placed Pratasevich under house arrest in an unknown location and likely tortured him.

In a playbook later copied by American governors Greg Abbott and Doug Ducey (as we'll see in Chapter 6), the Lukashenka regime sent thousands of migrants, mostly from Iraq, from Belarus to the borders of the European Union. Both Polish and Belarusian authorities used tear gas and water cannons against the migrants, who were left in freezing temperatures without adequate shelter, supplies, and assistance. At least twelve people died in the cold.

Poland

Poland's rightwing populist president, Andrzej Duda, won a second five-year term by a razor-thin margin in 2020. He ran on his nationalist promise to "re-Polandize" the Polish media and exert control over foreign-owned businesses in Poland. Against a backdrop of tens of thousands of white Polish nationalists chanting, "Pure Poland. White Poland," Duda's campaign was dominated by cultural issues, including homophobia and anti-Semitism. By denouncing gay rights, Duda sought the approval of the religious right. And in a country that once held Europe's largest Jewish community before it was decimated in the Holocaust, Duda's anti-Semitic comments are clearly divisive. There is similarity between Duda and his ally Trump, who welcomed Duda to the White House in the month before the Polish election and announced to the world that Duda was doing a "terrific job." And, like the United States, Poland is deeply divided. Duda is backed by the ruling rightwing Law and Justice party, and despite a Catholic tradition of support for immigrants, this party in this largely Catholic country is notable for its opposition to immigration. Duda's authoritarianism is reflected in his leverage over the media and the justice system, and his oppression of the

LGBTQ community has reached a point that many are leaving the country. Most recently, there is concern that Polish historian, Barbara Engelking, may be censored by government entities for her outspoken comments on the role of Poles during the Holocaust.

Slovenia

Slovenia is Hungary's neighbor, and until his recent election loss, Prime Minister Janez Janša had pledged to bar asylum seekers from the Middle East to "ensure the survival of the Slovenian nation." He was charged with trying to "Orbanise" Slovenia by cracking down on the media and the press. Slovenian historian Luka Lisjak Gabrijelcic says of Janša, "His base supports him but lots of people really hate him." Gabrijelcic said he quit Janša's party because it "turned too nasty."[10]

Janša was recently replaced by Prime Minister Robert Golob, who unlike Janša is a progressive supporter of the welfare state, democracy, the European Union, and protection of the climate.

THE DEVELOPING WORLD

In the developing world of Africa, Asia, and Latin America, there are varied forms of populism, nationalism, and authoritarianism, just as there are immense variations between the people and cultures of countries within these regions. Perhaps the most prominent among the populists are former Brazilian President Jair Bolsonaro, Prime Minister Narendra Modi of India, and Julius Malema in South Africa.

Brazil

Brazil's former rightwing President Bolsonaro has been called the "Brazilian Trump," and he campaigned for the presidency on the slogan "Brazil First." Pope Francis has been especially concerned about the impact of commercial activities harming the environment of the Amazon, as well as the indigenous people who live there. He spoke out against those who are, with a "blind and destructive mentality," destroying the Amazon rainforest,[11] to

10. Higgins, "Populist Leaders in Eastern Europe."
11. Pope Francis, in Phillips, "Bolsonaro Targets the Catholic Church."

which Bolsonaro responded: "Brazil is the virgin that every foreign pervert wants to get their hands on."[12] Despite his colorful, though very inappropriate verbiage, his policies have worsened the deforestation of the Amazon, harmed the Amazon's Indigenous people and their cultures, and triggered an authoritarian-inspired breakdown of Brazil's democracy. In 2022, former President Lula de Silva won the presidential election, and the world is waiting to see if his leftwing government can bring improvements to the Brazilian people and protection to the rain forest.

Unfortunately, Brazil is taking a page from the U.S. right, as supporters of Bolsonaro attacked police on the day authorities certified the victory of Lula da Silva. Bolsonaro supporters set fire to cars and buses after trying to invade the federal police headquarters. Although he has not blocked the handover of power, Bolsonaro has refused to concede defeat. Some supporters have camped outside army bases urging the military to overturn the result of October's presidential vote, citing conspiracy theories that the election was stolen. The former president has barely spoken in public since losing to Lula de Silva and has since traveled to the United States. His next moves are uncertain.

India

India's Prime Minister Narendra Modi represents the Bharatiya Janata Party (BJP), which is a Hindu nationalist party. In many ways, Hindu nationalism is like white Christian nationalism and can be just as extreme. And the slogan, "Hindu First," sounds eerily similar to "America First," except that it includes the religious component. Like Donald Trump, Modi's government has engaged in protectionism by raising tariffs on imports and encouraging Indians to buy local products rather than imports. There is lingering to public anger at Modi for the enormous wave of coronavirus deaths and a struggling economy, though he continues to be easily reelected.

Hindu nationalism is premised on the notion that those who view India as the "fatherland" are the "pure people." These include Hindus, Sikhs, Jains, and Buddhists, but not Christians, Jews, and most notably, not Muslims. Underlying this is the view that India had a glorious past that was destroyed by Muslim and Christian invaders, and since its independence in 1947, it has been held back by corrupt elites linked to neighboring Islamic Pakistan.

12. Bolsonaro, in Phillips, "Bolsonaro targets the Catholic Church."

Modi's most alarming recent policy is the 2019 Citizenship Amendment Act, which contains two controversial policies. First, the legislation gives Indian nationality to undocumented non-Muslim immigrants from Afghanistan, Bangladesh, and Pakistan who came to India due to religious persecution. These include Hindus, Sikhs, Buddhists, Jains, Parsis, and Christians. Muslims, however, are not included and undocumented Muslim immigrants are deported. Despite international objections, India recently deported a group of Rohingya refugees back to Myanmar where they face horrible persecution. On the other hand, some Indian citizens do not want Indian citizenship granted to any refugee or immigrant, regardless of their religion, as they fear it would alter the demographic balance and trigger a loss of Indian culture, land, and political rights. They also fear it will encourage more immigration from Bangladesh.

The second part of the legislation is the creation of a National Register of Citizens as an official record of all legal citizens of India. Protesters view this as authoritarian, and the police have cracked down on university students protesting it.

Lastly, India is heading down a road in the education of children that sounds uncannily similar to parts of the United States, most notably Florida. Florida Governor Ron DeSantis is restricting schools in teaching subjects such as the U.S. slavery, native American genocide, and issues pertaining to LGBTQ people. President Modi is similarly trying to whitewash Indian history, deleting Muslim contributions to the nation, and ignoring issues like caste discrimination in the Hindu caste system.

South Africa

South Africa's President Cyril Ramaphosa, who came to power in 2019 as head of the African National Congress (ANC), is popular. He handled the coronavirus pandemic quite well, is the current chair of the African Union, and leads Africa's engagement with the World Health Organization. However, this section is not about him. It is about his opponent, Julius Malema, also called "Juju." Once a member of the ANC, Malema formed a new party called the Economic Freedom Fighters in 2013 and became the party's leader. The Economic Freedom Fighters presents itself as a "radical, leftist, anti-capitalist and anti-imperialist movement." Its platform includes the nationalization (government ownership) of mines and banks and the expropriation of land for redistribution. It also calls for increased access to quality education, healthcare, and welfare services. It is particularly supported by young people, the poor, and the unemployed.[13]

Julius Malema has been a relentless opponent of South African inequality and the country's failure to redistribute land from the white minority to the black majority. In 2016, he warned that the land would be taken by any means necessary, though he later clarified that he was not calling for the "slaughtering" of white people. Malema's politics have been referred to as populist, but this example of populism is at the left end of the spectrum, as opposed to those on the right.

QUESTIONS FOR DISCUSSION

1. Contrast European nationalist movements with nationalism in the United States.

2. Contrast Western Europe with Eastern Europe in their nationalistic populist movements and leadership.

3. Compare Jair Bolsonaro with Donald Trump? Why do you think the two men are so similar?

4. How does India's Hindu nationalism compare with U.S. white Christian nationalism?

5. How does South Africa's background with apartheid affect its politics today?

13. McKenna, "Economic Freedom Fighters."

Knowing the Discarded

Chapter 5

The Discarded in America

MULTIPLE GROUPS OF PEOPLE and countless individuals are discarded everyday by populist ideologies, and many more are exploited by unrestrained capitalism. ("Discarded" and "exploited" are the terms used by the pope, and together, they represent "the marginalized" people.) Many others are simply ignored in a world where their pain and suffering are not the priorities of their leaders or their fellow human beings. These next four chapters cover four groups, each separately: those discarded by populism in the United States, those discarded by populism in the rest of the world, those exploited by unrestrained capitalism in America, and finally, those exploited by unrestrained capitalism around the world. After each of these marginalized people or groups of people is discussed, we seek encouragement in "compassionate encounters." These encounters mimic the visits between Saint Francis and the Sultan and between Pope Francis and the Grand Imam referred to by the pope in *Fratelli Tutti*. We, in turn, use visits as metaphors for compassionate encounters that bring healing, though these encounters might cover a range of actual activities. They may be as simple as a visit between two people, or as complex as a call for a global peoples' movement. Some visits bring direct healing, and some take time. These compassionate encounters nevertheless give us hope that caring people will eventually make the situation better. In the aggregate, they will make ours a better world.

As we address the topic of Americans discarded by populism, we keep in mind that the discarded can include the populist leader's base of support, especially if supporters are manipulated by a leader who never truly cares about their needs. They can also include members of the "elite establishment," especially those who are honorable people but are treated dishonorably by populists and their followers. But the primary victims, the ones on whom we focus most of our attention, are the scapegoats blamed for the troubles of the populist's base. We also include other discarded people who are simply ignored because they do not catch the attention of a narcissistic leader or an uninformed and/or disinterested public. We will consider the stories of these discarded people. We begin with those in the United States in this chapter, and then the rest of the world in Chapter 6. Many of the discarded in the United States are people of color, whereas many of the discarded around the world are immigrants (often of color). In both cases, the discarded can often include the poor.

HONORED VICTIMS OF RACISM

The Tulsa Massacre

In 1921, one of the worst incidents of racial terror occurred in Tulsa, Oklahoma, when a white mob descended upon the Greenwood neighborhood, one of the country's most prosperous Black communities. The mob decimated the neighborhood, killing as many as three hundred people. To this day, there are only two remaining survivors of the massacre: 108-year-old Viola and her 102-year-old brother, Hughes.

Compassionate Encounters. In March 2023, Viola and Hughes became dual citizens of the African country of Ghana. This was in follow-up to their visit to Ghana in 2021 on the centennial anniversary of the massacre. At that time, the president of Ghana had invited all the African diaspora around the world to visit Ghana to mark the "Year of Return," commemorating 400 years since the first Africans arrived in the Virginia colony. The Ghanaian president announced, "This country is your country, and anyone who wants to come to re-establish, connect with us here, is welcome."[1] The trips by Viola and Hughes to Ghana were sponsored by the company, "Our Black Truth," suggesting the importance of truth-telling. We'll return to the concept of truth-telling at the end of the book. While in Ghana, Viola and Hughes placed their names on the Sandofa Wall, a memorial inscribed with the names of members of the visiting African diaspora.

---

1. President Nana Akufo-Addom, in Brown, "Tulsa Massacre Survivors Become Citizens of Ghana."

The meaning of all this, including the Ghanaian citizenship of Viola and Hughes, was clear. Ghana's ambassador to the United States said to Viola, "I now invite Queen Mother Naa Lameley Viola Fletcher to take the oath of allegiance." When the ceremony was over, Hughes said, "I feel like a king. It is an honor and privilege to be a member of Ghana."[2]

Would a universal opportunity for a visit to Ghana lead to widespread healing of African Americans? Could it be one of many forms of reparations?

The Bust of Thurgood Marshall

Imagine the experience of walking through our nation's Capital Building and seeing the memorial bust of Roger B. Taney, the U.S. Supreme Court chief justice who authored the opinion protecting slavery in the Dred Scott decision in 1857. Scott was a Black man born into slavery who sought to use the courts to gain his freedom. Taney rejected his plea, stating that,

> "People of African descent had for more than a century before been regarded as beings of an inferior order, and altogether unfit to associate with the white race, either in social or political relations; and so far inferior, that they had no rights which the white man was bound to respect."

He added that a Black person, "might justly and lawfully be reduced to slavery for his benefit."[3]

To read this is jolting, as it must have been for every Black person who read these words every time he or she walked past the bust of Taney.

Compassionate Encounters: Now a visit to the Capitol will be much more uplifting, for the bust of Roger Taney has been replaced by one of Thurgood Marshall. Marshall was an African American civil rights lawyer and jurist who eventually served on the Supreme Court. He was an honorable man. The text of the legislation authorizing this switch included the following words:

> "While the removal of Chief Justice Roger Brooke Taney's bust from the Capitol does not relieve the Congress of the historical wrongs it committed to protect the institution of slavery, it

2. Duncan-Smith, "This Country Is Your Country."
3. Sotomayor and Want, "House Votes to Remove Bust of Justice Taney."

expresses Congress's recognition of one of the most notorious wrongs to have ever taken place in its rooms."[4]

Amidst the rejoicing over the switch of the Capitol busts, there was also joy over the brand-new domestic mailing stamps with the face of John Lewis. John Lewis was a civil rights activist and member of Congress from Georgia until his death in 2020. The stamps now serve as a daily encounter that reminds us that John Lewis too was an honorable man.

The Gate of the Exonerated

Once known as the Central Park Five, five Black and Latino teenagers were exonerated of their convictions for the beating and rape of a white woman in Central Park, New York City, when another man confessed in 2002. After the high-profile 1989 assault of the jogger, police had sought to round up men and boys of color as suspects in the rape without attention to their legal rights. The Central Park Five had served six to thirteen years in prison by the time they were exonerated. Donald Trump played a role in advocating for the death penalty at the time of the five men's arrest.[5]

Compassionate Encounters: In late 2022, people gathered at the gate of Central Park to dedicate the entrance to the men now remembered as the Exonerated Five. It is called the "Gate of the Exonerated." According to one of the men who had gathered, "This is a moment. This is legacy time."[6]

The Award for Emmett Till

Emmett Till was a Black teenager in 1955, when he was charged with whistling at a white woman in a grocery store in rural Mississippi. Till was abducted from his bed, tortured, and killed by a white mob. Till had a courageous mother, Mamie Till-Mobley. Despite the horrible disfigurement of her son that stemmed from the beating, she insisted on an open casket. She wanted the world to see what was done to her son. The world indeed did see it when the photos were published in *Jet Magazine.*

Compassionate Encounters. As a result of the photos, a civil rights movement was galvanized. And in 2022, the U.S. House of Representatives

4. Bushard, "House Votes To Replace Bust."
5. Choiniere, "Central Park Five."
6. Shraffey and Calvan, "Central Park Entrance Honors."

unanimously voted to posthumously award the Congressional Gold Medal to Emmett and his mother. The medal will be placed in the National Museum of African American History near the display of the casket in which Emmett was buried. When the bill was introduced in the Senate, Senator Cory Booker stated, "The courage and activism demonstrated by Emmett's mother, Mamie Till-Mobley, in displaying to the world the brutality endured by her son helped awaken the nation's conscience, forcing America to reckon with its failure to address racism and the glaring injustices that stem from such hatred."[7] Emmett's death, and Mamie Till-Mobley's courage, played a role in eliciting compassion in a nation that previously seemed incapable of it.

Some might say that "returning to Ghana," replacing a bust, printing a postage stamp, naming a gate, and awarding a medal are pretty trivial in the scheme of things, especially in the context of overwhelmingly evil events of great magnitude. But sometimes we move forward with baby steps, while recognizing that these steps are big to some people. In their entirety, however, they are huge.

COLLEGE STUDENTS OF COLOR

Regent Steve Sviggum found himself swimming in controversy when he suggested the University of Minnesota's Morris campus is perhaps 'too diverse', and this could constrain enrollment by making prospective students 'uncomfortable.' Too diverse? White prospective students uncomfortable? On a campus with a relatively diverse student population that is nevertheless majority white? Haven't educators been trying to make college campuses more diverse? Haven't traditional white students missed out on a broader and more varied cultural education that comes with cohorts of color? Haven't students of color felt lonely and isolated for far too long?

An editor visited with students at the Morris campus after the regent's remark. It quickly became clear to the editor that the diverse students were the ones who felt uncomfortable, not the white students, despite the relatively high proportion of diverse students on the campus. When he requested student reactions to the regent's words, one Native American named Dylan said, "I have no . . . clue what that [too diverse] even means," and a Filipino student named Ryan responded, "I feel unsafe and unwanted. I feel like I don't belong." Another student named Matthew asked the question:

7. Amiri, "House Votes."

"What does he [the regent] want for our (campus) community? Wouldn't you want a diverse community?"[8]

Eventually students began revealing their deepest feelings. One young Indigenous woman named Mercedese told the editor she often feels alone on the campus and in this western Minnesota town. "I feel isolated," said Mercedese.

> "Before [the regent] said all of that I was going to my counselors and telling them I was having a hard time adjusting to being here . . . There are just a handful of Native students here and all from separate tribes . . . In several of my classes I'm the only person . . . maybe one other . . . person of color."[9]

The editor spoke to a Black student named Biruk, who admitted feeling isolated and alone.

> "It's absolutely absurd [the University is called] too diverse. It's the exact opposite . . . we definitely need more diversity. I've been the only Black student in most of my classes."

Regarding the regent, Biruk added, "It's scary that someone in power has that point of view." Another student named Dawson said, "That doesn't even make sense that a liberal arts school is 'too diverse.'"

Compassionate Encounters: As the editor continued to speak with the students, he found that despite a feeling of anger toward the regent, and despite feelings of loneliness and isolation, it was also clear there were strong bonds of friendship on the Morris campus. Biruk admitted that "the people here (on campus) are welcoming and I feel loved." And Dawson added:

> "We're unique here because we're so separated from the fast-paced world. Here it's who's around you; that's who you got. There's no Target or Walmart here to take my money so I'm forced to be here on campus with my friends; and that's not bad at all.

The editor then spoke with a young white man named Grant, who said, "Contrary to being the problem, UMN Morris' diversity was a selling point . . . I kind of knew it was a diverse school and that actually attracted me." He added, "here, half my friends are Native American."

---

8. Colbert, "Isolation And Feelings Of Being 'Unwanted.'"

9. All student comments are from Colbert, "Isolation And Feelings Of Being 'Unwanted.'"

What the editor discovered among these white and non-white students was a strong sense of friendship and commitment to diversity. These serve to soften the blows of isolation and loneliness.

POORLY EDUCATED PEOPLE OF COLOR

Aside from the issues of diversity in higher education (of which we have barely scratched the surface), there is a problem with the quality and equality of kindergarten through grade twelve (K-12) education in America. The quality of education is highly unequal, with generally inferior quality for the poor. In part because they have higher poverty rates, this also means poorer quality education for people of color. Poor education is caused by poverty, and poverty in turn is caused by poor education. The factors restricting the *quality* of education and the *equality* of education are institutionalized and systemic to our country.

First, poverty in and of itself is associated with lower educational achievement, even if other contributing factors are not present.[10] This is discouraging, because by itself, it would mean that throwing money at educational problems wouldn't entirely solve the problem. And whereas the real solution is to eliminate poverty, we are nowhere near there yet. Nevertheless, there are other problems with our educational system that can and should be addressed.

First, we've noted that race is a factor. Census data reveal that students of color have lower educational attainment than white children. For example, close to ten percent of Indigenous students drop out of high school, followed by eight percent of Hispanics and over six percent of Blacks. In comparison, the white high school dropout rate is approximately four percent. Other children also struggle with K-12 education, including children in homes where there are violence and addictions, as well as children in migrant and homeless situations.

Since poverty is an underlying factor among most of these, we need to understand why it is so important. First, the quality of public K-12 education depends on funding, most of which comes from local property taxes. Low property-value school districts bring in small amounts of property tax revenue for the funding of K-12 education. Unless there is supplementary

10. For example, Parrett and Budge, "How Does Poverty Influence Learning?" Low and Low, "Education and Education Policy." American Psychological Association, "Education and Socioeconomic Status."

funding by federal and state governments through various forms of equalizing formulae, low property-value school districts will provide a relatively poor-quality education. The equal opportunity we like to think is assured through education isn't so equal after all.

Next, children in poor K-12 schools struggle to graduate from high school, and even if they earn their high school degree, they may still fail to meet college admission requirements. Even if admitted, they may be unprepared to succeed in college. And all this presumes they can afford to go to college. Many cannot. Pell grants for low-income student college tuition have declined over time, and even if college were tuition-free, low-income students often cannot afford the opportunity cost of higher education (i.e., the forgone income from working full time work rather than attending school). Hence, it is no surprise that data reveal far fewer college, graduate, and professional degrees among students of color.

Additionally, we need to ask the question: how many well-meaning white parents, upon learning Black children will be joining their children's classrooms, complain to school boards, investigate private or charter school alternatives, and or resort to home-schooling their children? And just how adamant are they in favor of legislated vouchers that shift funding from public schools to private ones, including private schools that discriminate on the basis of race and religion? These practices are common among parents who insist they would never be racist.[11]

And finally, whereas affirmative action leads to charges of "reverse discrimination" by white families, and whereas the Trump administration filed court cases against affirmative action (soon to be decided by the Supreme Court), the real privilege occurs for white children, who are far more likely to be legacy students (with parents who attended their chosen college) or students whose parents make financial contributions to their college of choice. Today's college admission scandals are almost comic, given the huge legal advantages already available to white students.

Compassionate Encounters. Educational policy is complex, and solutions include a better means of financing public education, and of course, a reduction in poverty. But studies also reveal enormous benefits to children

---

11. The use of vouchers for private schools, including schools that discriminate by race and ethnicity, is promoted by Republicans. With the money following the student, public funds are shifted to private schools, and public schools receive even less funding than they do now. With the 2022 Supreme Court ruling that permits expanded public funding for private schools, we can expect that public schools, which are attended by most low-income children and children of color, will lose funding.

who participate in preschool, especially when these children are in some way disadvantaged. Preschool addresses problems directly attributable to poverty, as well as those caused by poor school funding and educational segregation. Unfortunately, while preschool programs such as Head Start are extremely cost-effective, their funding is insufficient to meet the needs of all children. President Biden's proposal for three years of free, high-quality preschool, failed to pass in Congress, especially due to the opposition of Republicans. This should be a priority. In the meanwhile, one partial solution that is readily available is *Sesame Street,* a television show that has been known and loved by children and their parents for decades.

New research has found that *Sesame Street* improves school readiness among children, and therefore leads to improved early educational outcomes. Boys and Black children experience the greatest improvements in school performance, and the beneficial effects are largest for children living in poor areas. The study concludes that *Sesame Street* is one of the largest and most affordable early childhood interventions ever to take place.[12]

Sesame Street has also helped children better understand and cope with childhood issues, including parental incarceration, addictions, and divorce; family homelessness refugee resettlement; grief, violence, and trauma; and other issues like foster care, racism, and autism. While perhaps not quite the same as the in-person preschool experience, *Sesame Street* certainly comes in a close second by bringing compassionate encounters and education to the living rooms of its young viewers.

POORLY HOUSED PEOPLE OF COLOR

Just as educational inequalities are systemic and structural, so too are inequalities in home and business ownership. Census data reveal homeownership rates by race and ethnicity, and the disparities are stark. Whereas almost three-quarters of non-Hispanic white people own their homes, only half or fewer of Black, Indigenous, and Hispanic people do. These disparities have widespread implications. Let's focus on African Americans, their history, and the repercussions of this history.

First, we know that many Black families left their homes behind in the south and headed north in a quest to escape Jim Crow laws and to seek better jobs. This was the first post-slavery step in the process of disenfranchising Blacks of their wealth, which largely consisted of their homes.

12. Levine and Kearney, "Early Childhood Education."

It didn't end there. Historically, the U.S. government refused to insure loans for the purchase of homes in desegregated areas. This resulted in banks requiring new white owners to sign racial covenants in which they agreed not to resell their home to Blacks. Additionally, the Department of Agriculture refused to lend to Blacks for the purchase of farms. (President Biden's proposal for reparations in the latter case was met with charges of "reverse discrimination.") Furthermore, banks are reluctant to lend money for the purchase of a home or business if the potential borrower lacks collateral, often in the form of home ownership, unless the borrower has other solid indicators of creditworthiness. However, even if African Americans meet the criteria for creditworthiness, the National Fair Housing Alliance has found that racially biased redlining continues to prevent Black housing loans to this day.[13] It has also been found that racial bias in appraisals and real estate agent behavior prevent Black integration into white neighborhoods, based on the very real expectation that white people do not want Blacks in their neighborhoods. In all these ways, discrimination in home and business ownership is part of our nation's fundamental structure.

And finally, along with restrictive housing covenants that prevent Black homeownership in certain geographical areas, zoning laws limit the construction of low-income and multi-family dwellings in suburban neighborhoods, effectively preventing most low-income Blacks from renting in these white neighborhoods. After all, in the minds of many suburbanites, low-cost multi-family structures are code for "Black housing," and Black housing is code for "crime." You may recall when Trump took his 2020 reelection campaign to the suburbs after reversing the Obama era affirmative action addition to the 1968 Fair Housing Act. Trump addressed the "Suburban Housewives of America":

> "I am happy to inform all of the people living their Suburban Lifestyle dream that you will no longer be bothered or financially hurt by having low-income housing built in your neighborhood."

Trump further ridiculed calls to "defund the police" and promised suburban women continued police protection with:

> "a wall of separation [from] the violent radical left, the Marxists, the anarchists, the agitators, [and] the looters.[14]

---

13. The National Fair Housing Alliance, http://www.nationalfairhousing.org.
14. Trump, Jul 28, 2020, in Stuart, "Trump Is Happy to Inform Suburban Voters."

While 'white suburban housewives' may deny they are racist, they may nevertheless fight to keep in place the zoning laws that prevent the construction of low-cost multi-family dwellings in their neighborhoods.[15] They may have similar attitudes regarding policing and educational segregation.

Lack of wealth in the form of a home has other significant implications. Without a home, African Americans lack the collateral and credit-history necessary for borrowing for a small business, for housing repairs, or to help their children become homeowners. It also makes it more difficult to get through tough financial times caused by the normal crises of life such as unemployment, illness, or pregnancy, since renters cannot do as homeowners do and take out a home equity loan. Without this option, eviction and homelessness are far more likely.

The Census Bureau data do show a high degree of segregation between the different races, and the National Fair Housing Alliance has found numerous deficiencies in segregated neighborhoods populated by people of color, including the following:[16]

- 33 percent fewer traditional banking institutions but twice as many alternative banking establishments (such as payday lenders charging enormous interest rates),

15. Betsy Hodges was the Democratic mayor of Minneapolis from 2014 to 2018. She wrote the following in an article for the *New York Times*. "The gaps in socioeconomic outcomes between white people and people of color are by several measures at their worst in the richest, bluest cities of the U.S. How could this be? . . . I can say this: White liberals, despite believing we are saying and doing the right things, have resisted the systemic changes our cities have needed for decades. . . . In Minneapolis, the white liberals . . . were very supportive of summer jobs programs that benefited young people of color. [But] I also saw them fight every proposal to fundamentally change how we provide education to those same young people . . . White liberal people in blue cities implicitly ask police officers to politely stand guard in predominantly white parts of town . . . and to aggressively patrol the parts of town where people of color live—where the consequences of bad policing are fear, violent abuse, mass incarceration and, far too often, death . . . Sustainable transformation of policing will require that white people of means disinvest in the comfort of or status quo . . . It will mean organizing for structural changes that wealthy and middle-class whites have long feared—like creating school systems that truly give all children a chance, providing health care for everyone that isn't tied to employment, reconfiguring police unions and instituting public safety protocols that don't simply prioritize protecting white property and lives." (Cited by Betsy Hodges, "As Mayor of Minneapolis, 'I Saw How White Liberals Block Change,'" *The Minneapolis Star Tribune*, Jul 10, 2020.)

16. National Fair Housing Alliance, http://www.nationalfairhousing.org.

- 38 percent fewer healthcare providers, including doctors, hospitals, clinics, and pharmacies, and

- 34 percent fewer healthy lifestyle amenities such as parks, playground, and recreation centers.

Lastly, some segregated neighborhoods experience extensive gun violence. Marcus Hunter was a Black teenager living in Minneapolis. He was a different kind of crime victim and wrote a newspaper editorial that includes this excerpt.

> " I live in a cemetery, with trees as tombstones . . . Families visit these trees as you would visit the grave of a loved one . . . When I look at a tree, I can imagine my name and a picture of my face on it with a balloon."[17]

Compassionate Encounters. When I read Marcus's editorial, I immediately knew he was gifted. I knew I would want to quote him, and I contacted him for permission. As it turns out, Marcus Hunter's story has not gone unnoticed. His college-coaching team created a "Go Fund Me" page as a way to raise awareness about Marcus's powerful writing and to create a college fund to compensate Marcus for his important work.[18] Within months, tens of thousands of dollars were raised, and Marcus was accepted into multiple universities. He decided to double-major in Business and Journalism and next he will earn his MBA. He continues to give back to his community through his writing, managing a youth gospel band, and mentoring his peers to pursue their dreams—despite the odds. According to Marcus,

> "The shock value [of GoFundMe] was great, actually . . . It excited me because I'm grateful just to see the support and how my writing has resonated and the outreach that it has brought upon everyone."[19]

His writing *has* resonated. We can only imagine how many young people are inspired to pursue their dreams because of Marcus. And we can only hope that many of them will choose to write, educate, and inspire others as a result.

---

17. Hunter, "I Live in a Cemetary."

18. Go Fund Me, The Coaching Team College Fund for Marcus Hunter.

19. Hunter, "I'm Grateful Just To See The Support," in Go Fund Me, The Coaching Team College Fund for Marcus Hunter.

THE HOMELESS

Closely linked to housing issues is homelessness. There are many reasons for homelessness, including situation where young people are driven away from home due to their behavior (addictions, violence, and so on) or their status (LGBTQ or otherwise non-conforming). However, it is much more common to find that homelessness arises due to foreclosure or eviction, or simply insufficient funds to pay for housing. Once homeless, it is nearly impossible to find a job, maintain one's health, and assure any sense of safety or security.

Our nation has failed over many years to meet the housing needs of the poor. Our two principal housing policies, Section 8 Housing and public housing, have been underfunded for decades, leaving years-long waiting lists for some poor people and their children. In addition, public housing concentrates poverty and the distress that accompanies it.

While data on homelessness are limited, in part because definitions of homelessness vary, the National Alliance to End Homelessness reports that families with children make up 33 percent of the homeless.[20] These families are typically headed by young, single, and poorly educated women. Furthermore, people of color have far higher rates of homelessness than whites.

Homelessness has a negative impact on children's education, health, sense of safety, and overall development. It has been shown that homeless children 1) have higher levels of emotional and behavioral problems, 2) are at increased risk for serious health problems; 3) have a greater likelihood of separation from their families; and 4) experience more school mobility, repeat a grade, are expelled, drop out of school, and have lower academic performance.[21]

Homelessness worsened amidst COVID-19, especially among poor families with children. Even after the federal government responded to the crisis by imposing an eviction moratorium, this didn't solve the long run problem, which was high housing costs relative to incomes.

Sadly, there is considerable contempt for the homeless. This is especially evident in hate crimes. These are a few graphic examples:[22]

20. National Alliance to End Homelessness, http://www.endhomelessness.org.

21. National Alliance to End Homelessness, http://www.endhomelessness.org.

22. Stoops (ed.), "Vulnerable to Hate," and Matthew, "Crimes Against the Homeless Have Risen."

- A homeless man was repeatedly and deliberately driven over by an individual driving a car.

- A homeless man died following a brutal attack by three teenagers, who beat him with sticks and their fists.

- A 71-year-old homeless veteran was found lying in the street bleeding and unconscious after being stabbed more than 70 times by 21-year-old man. He died several days later.

- A homeless man was brutally beaten to death by a 20-year-old man and a 15-year-old boy.

- A 47-year-old homeless woman was beaten to death by a parolee registered as a sex offender.

Compassionate Encounters. Even though Touche was homeless in Minneapolis, he always tried to protect others on the street. When he heard about the new low-income housing construction taking place next to the homeless encampment called the Wall of Forgotten Natives, he went there—not to live—but to work. He was homeless, yet he worked for the homeless. On Thanksgiving Day 2020, Touche assisted a group of people handing out free meals, but first he fixed a plate and gave it to a woman he had seen sitting on an apartment stoop on his way to the meal give-away. He told her, "I just want you to know that I care about you because I've been where you're at." This homeless man met the needs of a stranger he visited, and he met the needs of the homeless not unlike himself.[23] Sometimes we wonder. Must a person be homeless to care about the homeless? Must a person be hungry to care about the hungry? If true, it is a sad commentary on those of us with nice homes and plenty of food.

Finally, recall we raised the issue of parents forcing their LGBTQ children to leave home. Pope Francis told such a group of parents, "God loves your children as they are" and "the church loves your children as they are because they are children of God." He also repeated his previous comments that parents should never force their LGBTQ children out of their homes.[24]

23. Otárola, "Once Homeless."

24. Pope Francis, "God Loves Your Children," in O'Connell, "God Loves Your Children."

THE ILL

First, some general considerations. Access to healthcare largely hinges on insurance coverage, and average life expectancy is an outcome of healthcare access. We see clear disparities in both, where, for example, over eleven percent of Blacks are uninsured, compared to just over seven percent of non-Hispanic whites. This contributes to a situation where non-Hispanic white people live on average five years more than Blacks! These disparities were in play before, amid, and since the coronavirus pandemic.

Nevertheless, COVID-19 caused large-scale illness and death across the globe, as well as in the United States. In America, just over one million people died of the virus, and many more were sick. Some people suffered disproportionately due to social conditions (as opposed to factors like old age). These include people ordered to work in unsafe but "essential production," people with no financial alternatives to working unsafely, those who used crowded and unsanitary mass transit to get to work, people in prisons and nursing homes, and people of minority race or ethnicity.[25]

Unfortunately, mental health suffered along with physical health during the pandemic. Many people lost access to therapy and support groups, and their mental illness and/or addictions became active once again. As the mental health of adults deteriorated, children's mental health was affected as well.

Children have been enormously stressed. Young children picked up the anxiety and fear of the adults around them, but lacked the skills and knowledge to understand and cope with what was happening. At the height of the pandemic, children couldn't play with friends, visit grandparents, or go to school or playgrounds. They heard words like "coronavirus" or "COVID-19" but didn't understand what they meant. And in some cases where the adults in their lives became severely stressed, children became witnesses to domestic violence and abuse. Fortunately, there are some resources to help.

Compassionate Encounters. Among the many online sources of help for children coping with the stress of the pandemic is *Sesame Street,* once again demonstrating it can be a "visitor" to a child's living room that can help with coping and healing. Its "Caring for Each Other" initiative has content to help families stay physically and mentally healthy during community-wide illness, including animated programs on healthy habits (such

25. Brux, *COVID-19 Series.*

as Elmo's "Washy Wash" song, instructions on sneezing hygienically, and ways to care for each other). In addition to information, resources provide comfort, and messages of love, kindness, and fun; and they are regularly posted on *Sesame Street* social media channels. *Sesame Street's* website includes child-friendly explanations to tough questions, and ways to help everyone stay healthy. There are self-care tips for caregivers, as they need to take care of themselves so that they are able to care for the children.[26]

Another place to visit is the Center for Disease Control.[27] It provides advice, aid, and resource links, including those for children and parents. For suicide prevention and mental health emergencies, call 988; for domestic abuse, call 1–800–799–7233; for addictions, call 1–800–662–4357, and for other emergencies, call 911.

VICTIMS OF CRIMINAL INJUSTICE

Incarceration

The 1994 U.S. Crime Bill generated mass imprisonment of Blacks for drug crimes, thereby creating a new form of slavery in the zero- or low-wage jobs performed by prisoners. Black cocaine users are more likely to use crack cocaine, whereas white users disproportionately use powdered cocaine. Both drugs cause harm, but crack cocaine carries far more severe penalties. Furthermore, when examining all types of crime, the data show Blacks are disproportionately arrested, serve disproportionately longer sentences, and have a disproportionately greater likelihood of receiving a wrongful conviction when compared to white people. For example, African American and East African drivers in Minneapolis account for 78 percent of minor traffic stops in which the officer searches the vehicle, whereas whites make up just twelve percent of similar stops and searches. This is despite far more whites being arrested.[28]

Furthermore, U.S. prisons are dangerous and traumatic places for prisoners. Many prisoners face strip searches and solitary confinement. Others face violence and live in crowded and unsanitary conditions. Prisoners have been found to have lower rates of vaccination and higher rates of COVID-19, such that the high rate of imprisonment among Blacks is one

26. Sesame Street, http://www.sesamestreet.com.

27. Center for Disease Control (CDC), www.cdc.gov/coronavirus.

28. Mannix, "Traffic Stops Criticized."

of the reasons for the excessively high Black COVID-19 infection and death rates. Furthermore, many prisoners have been found to have low abnormally levels of intelligence, higher rates of mental illness, and a history of childhood abuse. Many were young at the time they committed their crime.

Compassionate Encounters. The man became a symbol of hope. It happened after he was visited by a reporter while in prison who asked him about his conviction in a fatal shooting of an eleven-year-old girl. The reporter wrote that while the girl's death enraged the public, no one seemed to realize that the convicted man was just a boy, sixteen years of age, when sentenced to life in prison. In the years since the 2002 sentencing, research has revealed differences in the brains of adolescent children and adults, differences that reduce the culpability of a child. And further examination of the boy's conviction revealed several disturbing and probably racist practices, including failures in collecting evidence and lapses in questioning witnesses. The boy maintained his innocence and there was no evidence with which to identify him as the shooter. There is now a fundamental recognition that the boy's exceptionally long sentence was vastly unjust. The boy, now a man of 34 years, was released from prison in December 2020 after serving one-half of his life there. If not for the reporter's visit and story, the man who was convicted as a child would still in prison.

Indebtedness

Our legal system raises state revenue through fines, fees, restitution, and bail money. These pile up as debts among low level offenders and become immensely burdensome for those who are poor. Some borrow from payday lenders charging exorbitant interest rates, setting off a cycle of borrowing and debt. Because of these, the poor, including people of color, are more likely to be held in jail and prison than those with higher incomes.

Compassionate Encounters. Lexington County, South Carolina, recently reached a settlement with five people who had been jailed for failure to pay court fees and fines. These penalties had been imposed largely for minor traffic offenses. The five people were jailed for a length of time ranging between twenty and sixty-three days because they could not pay amounts ranging from $680 to $2,163. Four of them lost their jobs due to their jail time, rendering them even less capable of making their payments. Part of the problem was the county's insufficient number of defense attorneys and the lack of representation for the jailed defenders. This will now be remedied by increased numbers of Lexington County legal staff and higher pay for them. According to one plaintiff in the case, "The changes in this settlement are a long time coming, and I am so happy that this means more people will have meaningful access to counsel."[29]

The Death Penalty

Blacks and other people of color are disproportionately more likely to receive the death penalty than whites. Indeed, there is a long history of racial disparity in its application, and some people see a close connection between the lynching of Black men and the advent of the death penalty itself. As for the form of the death penalty, former President Donald Trump announced his intention to expand federal capital punishment protocols to include execution by firing squads and poison gas. In the context of grow-ing neo-Nazi movements, these graphics are especially alarming. In mid-2020, Trump ordered the first public execution in almost two decades, and just before leaving office, he speeded up the execution of thirteen death row inmates, of whom six were Black and one was Native American.

Compassionate Encounters. Bryan was a second-year law student when he visited a man on death row. According to Bryan,

> "they brought this man in, and he had chains everywhere. And they unchained this man. And I got so nervous that, when he walked over to me, I just said: "I'm so sorry. I'm just a law student. I don't know anything about the death penalty . . . but they sent me down here to tell you that you're not at risk of execution any time in the next year."

The man grabbed Bryon's hands and said, "Thank you, thank you, thank you," and then the man began to sing. Bryon said, "I couldn't believe how, even in my ignorance, just being present, just showing up could make a difference in the quality of someone's life . . . it taught me . . . about being present, about proximity." He added,

> "in that instant, [it was] so clear to me that we are all more than the worst thing we have ever done. . . . if someone tells a lie, they're not just a liar, . . . if someone takes something, they're not just a thief, . . . even if you kill someone, you're not just a killer."[30]

29. Marchant, "South Carolina County Settles Lawsuit."
30. Corrigan, "We Are All More Than The Worst Thing We Have Ever Done."

Botched Executions

The number of botched executions has reached an "astonishing" level, according to research conducted by the Death Penalty Information Center. By mid-December of 2022, seven of the year's twenty execution attempts, or 35 percent, were "visibly problematic," according to the report, either as a result of executioner incompetence, a failure to follow execution protocols, or defects in the protocols themselves. According to the Center,

> "After 40 years, the states have proven themselves unable to carry out lethal injections without the risk that it will be botched."
> The Center maintains that the families of victims and prisoners, other execution witnesses, and corrections personnel should not be subjected to the trauma of an execution gone bad.[31]

According to the Center, from 1972 through 2022, 90 men and women who were sentenced to the death penalty were later exonerated. Execution is irreversible, which is one of many good justifications for ending the death penalty.

Compassionate Encounters. The U.S. population is increasingly opposed to capital punishment. Polls in 2022 showed that support for the death penalty remained near historic lows, even amid rising perceptions of crime. One poll found that Americans' support for the death penalty was even lower when defendants had severe mental illness, brain damage, intellectual impairment, and military-related post-traumatic stress disorder. This is important, since the vast majority of those executed in 2022 were individuals with serious vulnerabilities, including well over half who had experienced chronic serious childhood trauma, neglect, and/or abuse. Many others, including Bryan, the young man we were introduced to moments ago, were not fully culpable of their crimes due to their young age.

Black Lives Matter

Finally, as we well know, Blacks have been systematically killed and injured by white police and white vigilantes. While George Floyd, killed in Minneapolis in 2020, is most notable, we know there have been so many more. We will address this later in the book.

---

31. The information and quotation in this section are from the Death Penalty Information Center, https://www.deathpenaltyinfo.org/.

QUESTIONS FOR DISCUSSION

1. Were you especially affected by any of the examples of discarded people? Why to you think this is the case?

2. Did any of the compassionate encounters have a greater impact on you than others? Why?

3. Do you believe that racism is systemic in the housing market? In education? In criminal justice? Please explain.

4. Did the issues involving COVID-19 resonate with you?

Chapter 6

The Discarded In The World

IMMIGRANTS

IMMIGRATION HAS BEEN A driving theme surrounding populism and its related ideologies, and immigrants have been among the primary scapegoats of populist leaders. Immigration issues are global in nature and have been addressed differently throughout the world. They are almost always highly charged situations, however, and often very dangerous for the immigrant. We first consider immigrants to the United States.

Immigrants to the United States

Republican governors Greg Abbott of Texas and Doug Ducey of Arizona sought to publicize their opposition to immigrants arriving from the southern border with what many have called a cheap political stunt. The immigrants were piled into buses and planes sent off to other states, not entirely unlike the immigrants sent from Hungary and Belarus to Poland, Lithuania, and Latvia. The immigrants to the United States were not given the opportunity for an informed consent for the bus and plane rides and, in fact, were manipulated for publicity for the governors. Many of the buses arrived in destinations in Philadelphia, Washington, D.C., New York City, and Chicago, along with their exhausted, confused, and frightened passengers.

Compassionate Encounters. Philadelphia is a sanctuary city in the truest sense. Mayor Jim Kennedy fought and won a major lawsuit against

Donald Trump's efforts to require local police to enforce federal immigration laws. Kennedy was also able to block access by Immigration and Customs Enforcement (ICE) to a Philadelphia data base that ICE was suspected of using to find undocumented people. Furthermore, the mayor barred city employees from asking residents about their immigration status. And finally, the mayor is bolstered by a wide network of immigrant rights groups that welcome arriving immigrants.

Peter is the co-director of one immigrant support group that has worked around the clock to help the newly arriving families. He states, "It is a clear and consistent message from the city of Philadelphia that immigrant communities are welcome here." Juan, the director of a different immigrant support group in Philadelphia, believes it is important that local residents are aware the immigrants are seeking asylum and have already been vetted by border authorities and legally permitted to move around in the country. Rather than dangerous criminals, they are ordinary families looking out for their kids. Laila, who works for the city of Philadelphia, states that, "If we had to uproot our lives and our families to create a better future, we would hope that others would treat us with dignity and respect." The attitudes and actions of the many community members and support groups serve to soften the abrupt landing of terrified immigrants into this great unknown. These immigrants are being cared for as if they were sisters and brothers.[1]

Immigrants to Canada

Mexicans, like Haitians and Central Americans from the Northern Triangle countries of El Salvador, Guatemala, and Nicaragua, are desperate to escape the gang violence that takes place in their countries at levels unimaginable to most of us in the United States. As noted previously, people are killed or kidnapped, as are their children, for things like witnessing a crime, refusing to pay bribes and protection money, and refusing to join a gang. Many of the migrants fleeing their homes have already lost family members to gang violence.[2]

Pedro, for example, lived in a Mexican city that had become a war zone, with guns shot, cars burned, and dismembered bodies left outside of schools on a regular basis. His wife, Rocio, is a 28-year-old lawyer who

---

1. Gammage and Conde, "Bused Migrants."

2. Stories and statements are based on Kamel, "More Mexicans Head to Canada," and Moses, "An Interview."

worked with abused women. When Rocio began receiving death threats from a drug cartel and the local authorities refused to help, the couple knew it was time to leave Mexico. "They knew where we lived and what car we drove," said Pedro. "Feeling like you are going to lose your life, or one of your daughters, I don't mind starting from scratch."

Others are fleeing political circumstances. One of these is Mexican immigrant, Viviana, who is a human rights activist and mother of four. She left Mexico after being attacked by the military. She said her work with families of missing and murdered women and girls made her a target. "Death threats were constant," she said.

Pedro, Viviana, their families, and countless other Mexicans have been desperate to flee their homeland but were deterred from seeking asylum in the United States by the harsh policies of Donald Trump and by a confusing and lengthy process that occurred under President Joe Biden's first half of his first term in office. In contrast, the asylum process in Canada is relatively straight-forward and easy. The odds are not necessarily better in Canada for successful outcomes, but the process and the wait time are often superior, and immigrants are aware of this.

For example, Pedro and his family heard the troubling stories of immigration in the United States. They knew about international treaties that supposedly protect people who are at risk, and that Canada abides by these treaties. They also hear stories of daily life in the United States. "The U.S. was never in our minds," said Pedro, "since there is a lot of violence . . . attacks where many innocent people die. Canada, statistically, has a very low rate of violence and its quality of life is better than the USA."

Similarly, Viviana was desperate to immigrate to Canada. "I thought it was the last option I had to be safe. I work for many causes and help many people. I did not want to stop helping, but I must protect [and] take care of myself."

The number of immigrants to Canada has been multiplying.

Compassionate encounters. It isn't just the relative ease of the asylum system that attracts immigrants to Canada. People like Pedro and his family are met by the Welcome Collective, which is a Montreal-based charitable organization that provides essential goods to new asylum-seekers. Similar programs offer welcome and assistance. For example, Viviana has been living in a women's shelter in Montreal since applying for asylum. These support groups make all the difference to traumatized strangers in unknown places.

There is another group of immigrants that seeks the protection of Canada. These are immigrants to the United States who are awaiting adjudication of their asylum claims. Many have been living with uncertainty about their status for many months or even years as U.S. caseloads have outweighed resources designated for responding to asylum claims. Some of these immigrants eventually feel they must move on, and they cross the unguarded portions of the Canadian border, often in the dark of night and the dead of winter. When arriving at the border, cold, hungry, and terrified, they are met by compassionate 'helpers,' who provide them and their children with warm clothing, blankets, and food. They then escape into the night and ultimately turn themselves into Canadian authorities as they seek asylum. Indeed, they have been met with compassionate encounters.

VICTIMS OF RACISM

In Brazil

In Recife, Brazil, the death of a poor Black child in the care of a rich white woman brought racism to the fore. In the early days of Brazil's coronavirus outbreak, when businesses and churches were closed, people stayed home if they could. But Mirtes continued to work as a maid, cooking, and cleaning for a wealthy family. One day Mirtes was required to leave the building to walk the family's dog, leaving her five-year-old son, Miguel, in the care of her boss, Sari. Sari left Miguel unattended inside an elevator, and the boy rode it to the top of the building and wandered outside. When Mirtes returned from the walk, she found him crumpled on the pavement outside the building. He had fallen nine floors and died. The alleged negligence of a wealthy white woman entrusted with a poor Black child helped kindle a nationwide reckoning over racism.

Racism is rampant in Brazil. More than 75 percent of the 5,800 people killed by police in 2021 were Black. Two-thirds of prison inmates are people of color and white people earn nearly twice as much as Blacks on average. Still, the Brazilian political right, including former President Jair Bolsonaro, insists that racism doesn't exist. According to Bolsonaro, "In Brazil, there isn't this thing of racism."

Compassionate Encounters. Demonstrators in Recife demanded justice for the death of Miguel. These protesters included many white people. Mirtes could scarcely believe it. In media interviews, she tied the treatment of her boss, who was released on a $4,000 bail, to a racial double standard. If Mirtes had been charged with the death of Sarí's son, she said, she wouldn't be free. To Mirtes, racism in Brazil has always been "discreet, subtle." Her boss had never said a racist word to her, but she knew of no other way to explain what had happened. "It was racism," she said. "It was prejudice against a maid's son."[3] As the last country in the Americas to abandon slavery, it should be no surprise that racism still exists in Brazil.

Sarí was charged with culpable homicide in Miguel's death. What happened next was a touching and compassionate encounter. Sarí asked for Mirtes' forgiveness in a public letter. "I have no right to talk of pain," she wrote in the letter. "But this weight, which is in no way comparable, will be with me the rest of my life." Perhaps her remorse helped ease Mirtes' pain. Perhaps the support Mirtes received from the protesters softened her pain as well.

Sarí's conversion coincided with a broader transformation in Brazil, a national reckoning of sorts. Spurred by the deaths of George Floyd in Minneapolis and Miguel in Recife, Brazilians are recognizing the structural nature of the country's racism. They are confronting it straight on in multiple ways, including their demand for the removal of a São Paulo statue of Borba Gato, a 17th-century settler who hunted and enslaved indigenous people as he expanded Brazil's territory. A brand of sponge whose name had been used to ridicule Afro-Brazilian hair has been taken off the market. A prominent news show convened its first-ever panel of exclusively Black journalists to discuss racism. And affirmative action is now being used to diversify the university student body.

On February 14, 2022, the Black Lives Matter flag was raised on the premises of the U.S. Embassy and Consulates in Brazil to commemorate Black History Month and to honor the birthday and life of anti-slavery activist Frederick Douglass. Victims of racism across the world can take some comfort from Black Lives Matter in Brazil, and in the formal apology not just by the rich woman Sari, but also the Dutch prime minister for the role played by the Netherlands in the global slave trade, which included Brazil.[4]

3. McCoy, "Prejudice against a Maid's Son."

4. Prime Minister Mark Rutte's apology was met with a mixed response. Many regretted that he didn't mention reparations.

In South Africa

South Africa experienced apartheid up until 1994 and continues to bear the inequities of that period. People's variations in skin color mean everything: their residence, privileges, hardships, and deprivation. Recently, forty-year-old Collins Khosa died in Alexandra, a poor township in Johannesburg, South Africa, after an altercation in his yard with security forces. They had accused him of drinking alcohol in public, which became an offense during emergency regulations put in place to prevent the spread of coronavirus. Witnesses say soldiers and police officers strangled Khosa, slammed his head against a cement wall and a steel gate, and hit him with the butt of a rifle. Afterward, Khosa couldn't walk or talk. He began vomiting. A few hours later, he was dead. A postmortem report described the cause of death as "blunt force head injury." The government blamed Khosa for the initial disturbance and denied that his beating had caused his death.

Khosa's widow, Nomsa, said she doesn't understand all the legal procedures involved in the case. But she no longer trusts the army and police. "Collins is gone; he's not coming back," she said.[5]

Compassionate Encounters. When South Africa's World Cup-winning former rugby captain Francois Pienaar recently went down on one knee in support of Black Lives Matter at a cricket event in Cape Town, worldwide victims of racism were heartened. Subsequently, Cricket South Africa ordered its players to take a knee before matches in support of the Black Lives Matter movement.

Nomsa is heartened by the support she is receiving from around the world. People are demanding justice for Collins, and there is a petition you can add your name to.[6]

MUSLIM MINORITIES

The Rohingya

Myanmar (formerly Burma) consists of many different ethnic groups, though the principal ethnicity is Buddhist. Buddhism, of course, is also a religion. The Rohingya are a minority Muslim group living in the western

---

5. Khosa, "Top of Form Report Clearing Soldiers."

6. *A Petition for Collins Khosa*, https://www.change.org/p/sandf-justice-for-collins-khosa.

state of Rakhine in Myanmar. In 2016, the Buddhist Myanmar military began an ethnic cleansing of the Rohingya, whom they claimed were terrorists that had stolen their land. They burned down Rohingya villages, raped Rohingya women, and killed their children. Matters worsened in 2021 when the military launched a coup. Since then, there has been guerilla warfare and civil unrest in many regions throughout the country. All in all, tens of thousands of Rohingya Muslims have been killed, and almost one million have been exiled to refugee camps outside Myanmar. The Rohingya are considered one of the world's most persecuted minority groups.

Compassionate Encounters. There is a village in Myanmar where Buddhists and Muslim Rohingya have been friends over many generations. Ethnic cleansing was expected to put an end to that, but that wasn't the case. Instead, women come together as women to help each other in their maternity.

A documentary telling the story of the village opens with a Rohingya woman giving birth. She is young and very weak, and it takes some time for the child to be delivered. Everyone breathes a sigh of relief when the baby is born alive. Hla, a Buddhist woman, is the founder and midwife of the clinic where the young Rohingya woman delivers her baby. Hla treats all pregnant women, Buddhists and Rohingya alike. Nyo is a Rohingya apprentice midwife. She is not permitted to treat Buddhists, but she works at the clinic, treating and translating for Rohingya patients. Her presence brings them great comfort.

In a conflict zone such as in Rakhine state, Buddhists and Rohingya Muslims are enemies. But in the villages where families live, women are more like sisters. They are healer and patient, midwife and apprentice. They work together to care for each other.

The director of this documentary states that when we think of violent conflict zones, we think of men as fighters and soldiers. But also in a conflict zone, "there are women, and there are children . . ." She dedicated the film to women in conflict zones.[7]

The Uighurs

One young Uighur woman escaped from an internment camp in Xinjiang province in northwestern China. Amid sobs and tears, she spoke about her experience to a reporter. She said the men came at night, always wearing

7. Hlang, "Midwives."

masks and suits. They would select the women they wanted and take them to a "black room." "Perhaps this is the most unforgettable scar on me for-ever," she said. "I don't even want these words to spill from my mouth." She was tortured and gang-raped on three occasions, each time by two or three men. "Police boots are very hard and heavy, so at first I thought he was beating me with something," she said. "Then I realized that he was tram-pling on my belly." She added, "They had an electric stick, I didn't know what it was, and it was pushed inside my genital tract, torturing me with an electric shock." The young woman continued to talk between sobs. "They don't only rape but also bite all over your body, you don't know if they are human or animal," she said in tears.[8]

This young woman is a member of an oppressed Uighur (pronounced wee-ger) Muslim minority group that represents almost half the population in China's Xinjiang Province. (The term "Uighur" is alternatively spelled "Uyghur.") The United States and many international human rights groups are calling the treatment of the Uighur population a genocide and are charging the Chinese with crimes against humanity. Millions of Uighurs have been forced by the Chinese government into 're-education camps' for political and cultural indoctrination. Abuses are alleged to be widespread, including gang rapes and torture.

China's birth control policies against minorities in Xinjiang are harsh, and they prevent millions of births through forced abortions and steriliza-tion. Experts refer to this as "demographic genocide." Mass surveillance is used to keep track of Rohingya people outside the camps, and Muslim traditions are banned. The goal of the Chinese is a cultural genocide along with the human one. Cruel Chinese policies have resulted in large numbers of refugees who escape to Afghanistan, Turkey, Bangladesh, and others. More recently, they have also migrated to Europe and the United States.

Compassionate Encounters. Frontline visited two Uighur sisters for preparation of a documentary entitled, "China Undercover."[9] This visit was part of a broader investigation into China's mass imprisonment of Uighurs and other Muslim minorities in the region of Xinjiang. Since the original broadcast, *Frontline* has received updates involving the two sisters featured in the documentary.

The two Uighur sisters—Gulzire, who is a refugee living in Germany, and Gulgine, who is a resident of Xingiang—made a plan. They agreed that

8. PBS Frontline, "China Undercover."

9. PBS Frontline, "China Undercover."

Gulgine would change her profile picture on social media every week. That would assure her sister that she was safe and well. One day, when her sister's profile picture changed to show a dark, half-shaded room, Gulzire grew concerned and started searching for her sister. She found out from a friend that her sister was "studying"—a code word for being held in one of Xinjiang's detention camps. Later, despite an announcement from the Chinese government that people in the camps had been released, Gulzire continued to worry, because her sister's social media profile had not changed.

Then Gulzire was surprised to receive a phone call from her sister. The two sisters proceeded to have a six-minute video visit. Gulzire recounted, "My sister said, 'I'm here, I'm safe' . . . Then I saw my sister, my mother and my father. I didn't see my brother. I asked about my brother, and my mother said he has a job. My sister said she is a teacher, and yeah, that she was good and healthy. But I couldn't ask where she has been for over two years."

Before the call ended, Gulzire's mother told her not to join any protests. "I realized someone must be monitoring them, so that's why their attitude went from very excited to very serious all of a sudden," Gulzire said. Since that call, Gulzire has not heard from her sister or any other family member again. She could sense they are still living in fear and are under constant surveillance. Nevertheless, she was happy to have spoken to her family and this gave her hope. The Frontline documentary could provoke all of us to care about this oppressed population and do what we can to educate others and raise the issues with our legislators. These would represent genuine compassionate encounters.

The Yazidis

The Yazidis are a religious minority in Iraq whose religion combines elements from Christianity and Islam. The extremist group ISIL had conducted years of a genocidal campaign against the Yazidis. Their atrocities included sexual violence, mass executions, forced conversions, and other crimes. Since ISIL's military defeat, victims and survivors continue to experience mental anguish after years of captivity and profoundly inhumane treatment. Countless more still struggle to come to terms with the loss of beloved relatives, or even entire families, and they remain displaced from their homes until the conflict fully ends.

Compassionate Encounters. Christian Ritscher of the United Nations visited Sinjar in May, where he sought to bring justice to the "brilliant" young Yazidis. He said,

> I was truly inspired by the steadfastness and the persistence of those young women and men, who have survived unimaginable horror, to come forward and speak up about the gravity of the brutalities that befell them, as well as their trust and belief in the path of accountability and justice.[10]

Ritscher added,

> The young women and men of the Yazidi community deserve to be recognized for what they have endured and continue to endure, yet their ability to rise, develop, and take their future into their own hands is genuinely impressive.[11]

Ritscher stressed that this momentum was inspired by the courage and resilience of Yazidis themselves, in Iraq and around the world. He added that the perseverance of Yazidi women and girls, in particular, and their determination for justice and accountability, is driving global efforts toward investigations.

THE UNEDUCATED

In Africa

The key to development is education, and the education of girls provides enormous social benefits to developing countries. Studies show that if a girl is educated and becomes a mother, she will have lower fertility, she will be better able to assure the survival of her children, and she will be more likely to assure her children, including her girls, become educated. Hence, the benefits of the education of girls are widespread and intergenerational.

Education for girls is limited in very poor countries, including many African ones. If families can afford to send only some of their children to school, they are more likely to send their boys, since girls may well marry and move to their husbands' villages. Boys, on the other hand, are more likely to support their parents as they age.

10. Sánchez, "UN Renews Commitment."
11. Sánchez, "UN Renews Commitment."

Compassionate Encounters. Women's microenterprise group lending projects have been found to be of enormous benefit to the education of children in East Africa, where virtually all women interviewed in a research study said they would use their earnings from their new microenterprises to assure education for their children. As the lead researcher, I visited women in the cities, slums, and countryside in Kenya and Uganda, and aside from making new friends, I was pleased to learn the importance these very poor women placed on the education of their children, including their daughters.[12]

In Afghanistan and Pakistan

In other countries, notably Afghanistan and Pakistan, girls are prevented from going to school by the Taliban. As Taliban authority has waxed and waned, girls have started and stopped going to school, and they risk their lives when they do go. Malala Yousafzai was one of these girls.

Malala Yousafzai was shot in the head by the Taliban for advocating for the education of girls. After Malala recovered, she became the youngest recipient of the Nobel Peace Prize, giving voice to girls around the world. "I come from a country that was created at midnight. When I almost died it was just after midday." I heard a recording of Malala's speech at the Nobel Peace Center in Oslo, which was inspiring to me. Malala also wrote a book about her experience, and it continues to inspire girls everywhere.[13]

Compassionate Encounters. With the recent takeover by the Taliban once again in 2022, girls over sixth grade are not permitted to go to school. But one day, several street children, including little girls, visited with a woman, Soraya, in a neighborhood park. As Soraya began to teach them, more people came, including women who could not read and write. Another visitor passed by, and as a generous benefactor, he rented a house for Soraya to teach in, which enabled her to teach teenage girls away from the eyes of the police. Soraya now has 250 students, and besides teaching them to read and write, she also teaches them to stand up for their rights. She believes the Taliban have not changed since the late 1990's, so she says, "These are the same Taliban, but we shouldn't be the same women of those years.

---

12. Brux, et al., "Microcredit in Uganda;" and Brux and Miller, "Microenterprise Credit."

13. Yousafzai, *I am Malala.*

We must struggle: by writing, by raising our voice, by any way possible."[14] Clearly, she leads these girls through her compassionate encounters with them, girls who would otherwise be victims of the Taliban.

THE ILL

Recent headlines read like these: "Tuberculosis Cases Rise Globally," Cholera Outbreaks Surge," and "Measles Outbreak Kills Children." COVID-19 is partly to blame, as parents resist taking their children to clinics for illnesses and vaccinations due to fear of the spread of COVID-19 and due to lockdowns. But by focusing on the coronavirus, we see there are other issues involved. For example, lies and conspiracy theories contribute to unhealthy behavior and reluctance to be vaccinated.

What is more is that on Christmas Eve 2020—when thoughts of the Christian faithful turned to Bethlehem—the *Washington Post* published an article explaining that Palestinians in Bethlehem and throughout the occupied Palestinian territories would not receive the COVID-19 vaccine until all Israeli citizens had received it.

Fast forward three months later to Easter 2021—and the thoughts of many once again turned to the Holy Land. But for some, the rise of hope in their souls was matched by a thud of sorrow in their hearts. Christianity's empty tomb was met with wooden caskets—the coffins of Palestinian children who had not yet received the coronavirus vaccine. This was brushed off by Israel's Health Minister, who said, "I don't think that there's anyone in this country . . . that can imagine I would be taking a vaccine from the Israeli citizen, and, with all the good will, give it to our neighbors."[15]

Well, yes, a lot of people might well imagine that, since vaccinating people in occupied territories is not a matter of good will but a matter of international law. Under Article 56 of the Fourth Geneva Convention, an occupying country has the duty to ensure "the adaption and application of the prophylactic and preventative measures necessary to combat the spread of contagious diseases and epidemics." This duty requires the Israeli government to purchase and distribute vaccines to the Palestinian population under its control.

---

14. Faiez and Alizai, "School in the Shadows." The teacher's name has been changed for her protection.

15. Toi, "Most People Will End Up Being Infected."

As a result of Israeli policy, the health pandemic in the occupied territories has reached disturbing proportions, with thousands of COVID-19 deaths in Gaza and the West Bank. Why does anyone in Israel have a greater right to life-saving vaccines than anyone in Palestine?

Of course, there is a broader question—one that Americans should ponder: why does anyone in America have a greater right to life-saving vaccines than anyone else in the rest of the world, especially those in the world's poorest countries? President Biden himself announced, "We're going to start off making sure Americans are taken care of first, but we're then going to try and help the rest of the world."[16]

What do we make of this? While we are not the occupiers of poor countries, we nevertheless benefit from their labor, their natural resources, and their exported goods. And just as there is a chasmic divide between the rich and the poor within the U.S., there is an even deeper divide between the rich and the poor countries of the world. Think about Yemen. Think about Afghanistan. Think about Haiti and Somalia. And think about Palestine.

The rich are no more deserving than the poor. European ancestry is no more deserving than Arabic or African. Christians and Jews are no more deserving than Muslims. The Holy Land is a microcosm of the world, where the poor are held in contempt and denied the life-saving interventions that go to those who are far richer and far more powerful.

Compassionate Encounters. COVAX is a global vaccination organization that is affiliated with the World Health Organization, UNICEF, and other institutions. Its goal is to ensure that all countries participating in COVAX have equitable access to COVID-19 vaccines. As of late 2022, CO-VAX had delivered 1.8 billion coronavirus vaccines to 146 countries.

UNICEF has long been active in delivering vaccines and related equipment to the farthest reaches of the globe. The organization procures over two billion doses of vaccines annually for routine immunization and outbreak response. It has helped reach more than 760 million children with life-saving vaccines over the last twenty years, preventing more than thirteen million deaths. In addition, by vaccinating health workers globally, UNICEF helps ensure that it is safe for children and their mothers to get the critical health care they need—vaccinations, treatment of malnutrition and deadly diseases such as malaria and diarrhea, and obstetric, prenatal, and post-natal care along with services for newborns. These are critical services

16. Reals, "Biden Pledges."

without which children's lives are placed at risk. COVAX goes a long way in compassionate encounters with the poor of the world.[17]

THE HUNGRY

The World Food Program (WFP) is the preeminent global organization for addressing world hunger. While hunger has been falling in recent decades, recent global conflicts and climate-related weather events have reversed that success. The WFP reports that in the year before COVID-19, the number of people on the brink of starvation went from 80 million to 135 million. As of 2022, the number was expected to sky-rocket to 270 million, and most of these are children.

Examples of child hunger abound. Children in Syria and Yemen are victims of poverty and unending war. Children in Lebanon suffer from an economic collapse. Climate-related locust invasions threaten crops in Congo, Sudan, Kenya, and other African countries. Tourism in Ethiopia and many Latin American countries, which normally produces up to half of foreign revenue, came to an end with the pandemic. Children often rely on a family member migrating elsewhere for work and sending home remittances, but these payments have plummeted due to massive unemployment amid COVID-19. Then there is the hurricane season that batters the Caribbean and Central America, and the drought and flooding seasons that arrive in South Sudan. On top of all of these, people living in crowded and unsanitary conditions, often without soap and water, become even more vulnerable to illness due to their malnutrition.

The widespread hunger of children is alarming, especially in a world where the rich cannot find enough ways to spend all their money. Even middle-income people engage in a level of consumerism that prevents them from sharing what they have. The entire problem seems overwhelming. There is a temptation to turn away, thinking that nothing we do can possibly matter. That is a mistake.

Compassionate Encounters. The WFP estimates that it costs about 50 cents per day to feed a Syrian child. It costs up to one-hundred times this amount for a child to migrate with his or her family to a refugee camp elsewhere in the world. Even when the price of food is high, it is cheaper than the alternatives.

17. UNICEF, https://www.unicef.org/.

The WFP is asking for billions of dollars from developed countries. This is the only way to avert famine, mass migration, and destabilization that will otherwise cost more in the long run. This is also how we engage with our shared global humanity. We can contact our legislators, urging them that, despite all the other issues, they must also respond to the needs of hungry children throughout the world. We are in an unprecedented time requiring unprecedented activism.[18]

VICTIMS OF POLITICAL INSTABILITY

In Haiti

Haiti is the poorest country in the Western Hemisphere. Statistics tell the story. Twenty-nine percent of the population lives below the global poverty line of $2.15 per day, over twenty percent of children under age five are malnourished, and 66 percent of urban populations live in slums. The maternal mortality rate of 480 means that for every 100,000 infants born, 480 women die for pregnancy related reasons.

Hunger has existed for decades in Haiti, and in some places, it is reaching famine-conditions for thousands of people. The country's largest slum, Cité Soleil, is adjacent to the capital city of Port-au-Prince. Here and elsewhere, thousands of children face hunger. Homes are mere shacks, pieced together by littered scraps of metal and cardboard. During the rainy season, children and their families struggle to survive as their homes are completely flooded. Streets become "rivers of trash," mingled with barefoot children.

Since the assassination of former President Jovenel Moïse in 2021, political instability has gutted the nation's services and gangs have stepped into the power vacuum. When gang wars occur, civilians are the victims. Recent gang wars have burned down entire neighborhoods. Families flee their homes, and they camp on the streets of Haiti's cities. Women are raped, and many others die. At times, gangs block the ports through which fuel enters the country and this turns a faulty power system into a crisis. A lack of fuel impacts almost everything. Gas stations close. Trash collection stops and garbage piles up in the slums. Water utilities no longer pump enough water and aid workers cannot bring in water to areas blocked by gangs.

18. www.senate.gov and www.house.gov.

Even in normal times, gang violence is rampant, and children lie in makeshift camps to recover from their gunshot wounds. Cholera is spreading, in part because of filthy conditions and partly because armed gang members prevent doctors from providing care. Things do not look any better for the near future.

Compassionate Encounters. Little Jameson sat by his mother and cried. He is not the only crying child in Haiti. A visit there by a *New York Times* journalist brought us news of this boy and other children from a country so close to us geographically yet so far apart in its poverty, violence, and disease. According to the journalist, Haiti is in the middle of a humanitarian disaster. Yet despite their pain, she found that regular Haitians feel a lot of solidarity with each other. "A lot of people will tell you that they survived with the help from their neighbors. One young woman told me she fled her house after neighbors told her that gang leaders were coming to rape her. People are helping each other survive."[19]

In Nagorno-Karabakh

Undoubtedly, few readers are aware of the people of Nagorno-Karabakh, or even the countries of Armenia and Azerbaijan. These two countries were at war in 2020, but signed a peace agreement that ended the fighting . . . until now. In November 2022, Azerbaijan attacked Armenia over what it called provocations. The two countries are at odds over the disputed territory of Nagorno-Karabakh, which is largely inhabited by ethnic Armenians, and its seven surrounding districts, originally inhabited by Azerbaijanis. Nagorno-Karabakh and the surrounding districts are located geographically between the two countries along their borders with each other. A threesome consisting of the United States, Russia, and France make up the Minsk Group, tasked with finding a peaceful solution. Yet Azerbaijan maintains that the Minsk Group is biased in favor of Armenia, and Azerbaijan has the support of a mix of countries including Kazakhstan, Belarus, Ukraine, Kosovo, Georgia, Cambodia, Palestine, Israel, and others. Among the differences between Armenia and Azerbaijan is religion—most Armenians belong to the Armenian (Orthodox) Apostolic Church, whereas most Azerbaijanis are Muslim.

Compassionate Encounters. The Prime Minister of Armenia and the President of Azerbaijan have now begun to meet over peace negotiations.

19. Sanon and Coto, "Cholera Outbreak."

Some progress is noticeable. The fact that dialogue continues is a positive sign of progress.

VICTIMS IN CONFLICT ZONES

In Ethiopia

Tigray is one of eleven administrative regions in Ethiopia, Africa's second-most populous country. Each region is mostly autonomous, with its own police force and militia. Regional governments are largely divided along ethnic lines, and long-standing tensions between regions have led to ethnic nationalist clashes.

Ethiopia itself is very poor. Twenty-seven percent of the population lives below the international poverty line, and 35 percent of children under age five are malnourished. These figures have undoubtedly worsened with the recent conflict.

With the election of Prime Minister Abiy in 2018, the Ethiopian National Defense Force took power over the previously dominant Tigray People's Liberation Front (TPLF), which had ruled the country for over thirty years. This lay the groundwork for the armed conflict between the two parties in Ethiopia's Tigray region. The Tigray conflict began in 2020, and has left hundreds of thousands of dead, caused the displacement of millions, and created a famine that is currently endangering the lives of many more.

Ironically, Ethiopia's neighbor to the north is Eritrea, and Prime Minister Abiy Ahmed won the Nobel Peace prize in 2019 for helping to end Ethiopia's twenty-year war with Eritrea. Eritrean forces have since joined in the military campaign in Tigray on the side of the Ethiopian government. All actors in the conflict have been accused of carrying out atrocities, but Eritrean forces have been linked to some of the most gruesome. In addition to perpetrating mass killings and rape, Eritrean soldiers have been found blocking and looting food relief in multiple parts of Tigray. Ethiopia's government has also been brutal, as exemplified by its troops burning a Tigrayan man alive. As of late 2022, a cease-fire agreement was reached in Tigray, but many question whether it will last.

Compassionate Encounters. A woman gave birth while running from war in northern Ethiopia. She encountered a woman who was eight months pregnant, and they visited and then helped each other. One woman was ethnic Tigrayan, and the other ethnic Amhara. They belonged to enemy ethnic groups at war, yet they chose sisterhood over death. After all, shared motherhood is far more important than tribal differences. The two women walked together, slept together, and sought hydration and food together in the desert. They said, "We don't know who is fighting us. We don't know who is with us or who is not with us. We don't know. When the war came, we just ran." The women didn't know who they were in the terms of the war, but they knew who they were as mothers and therefor as sisters.[20]

Another encounter of similarly important, though quite different consequences took place toward the end of 2022, when military commanders from Ethiopia and Tigray met in Nairobi and agreed to allow unhindered humanitarian assistance into the region. One week earlier, the two parties signed a truce and agreed to disengage in all military operations. There are hopes for additional meetings in subsequent months.

In Yemen

Yemen is a small, very poor country that lies along the southwest border of Saudi Arabia. Twenty percent of the population of Yemen lives below the international poverty line, and 37 percent of children under age five are malnourished. The United Nations has declared that Yemen has the world's worst humanitarian crisis. This is in large part due to Yemen's "proxy-war," meaning that outside countries are at war in Yemen over their own issues. These proxies are Iran on one hand and a Saudi Arabian-led coalition that includes the United States on the other. In other words, Iran is fighting against the Saudi-led coalition on Yemen's soil. The people of Yemen are not interested in the objectives of Iran or the Coalition; they merely want to live and take care of their families.

People are dying from the bombs, but even more are dying from starvation and the largest known cholera outbreak because ports providing food and medicine are cut off from the people. We've seen photos of starving children before in the 1970s "world food crisis" in Africa's Sahel region and the 1972 famine in Bangladesh. Now, the photos show starving children in Yemen. The first time we see the photos, we know these children are suffering. The second time we see the photos is after the children have died. Over 10,000 children have died from starvation and disease.

---

20. Abulgasim and El-Mofty, "We Don't Know Who is Fighting Us."

Compassionate Encounters. At this River Falls, Wisconsin candle-light vigil, we quietly speak for Yemen's children:

> Hundreds of thousands of Yemen's children have died, many more are maimed, and millions more are malnourished. Yemen has the largest humanitarian crisis in the world—and children are being robbed of their futures. We urge our government to pull our military out of the conflict and engage in reconstruction and poverty relief instead.[21]

In Syria

Syria is still a conflict zone. Syrian children live and die from bombs that never seem to cease. They huddle with families and friends in basements, day-in and day-out, seeking protection from the bombs raining down on their homes. What appears to be a civil war is in reality, like in Yemen, a proxy war. The brutal leader, President Bashir al Assad, has the support of Russia and Iran, and according to the United Nations, over 300,000 Syrian civilians have died since the war commenced over a decade ago. One Syrian child captivated the world with her Twitter account, which included such comments as, "I'm very afraid I will die tonight . . . Stop killing us . . . I just want to live without fear." Seven-year-old Bana gave a voice to millions of innocent Syrian children.

Compassionate Encounters. After Bana Alabed and her family escaped from Syria, Bana's Twitter account was rewritten into a book. In the book, Bana doesn't merely tell the story of the war and its violence, but she also gives the world reason to hope. She calls for peace and an end to all global conflict. When she grows up, she would like to become a teacher. She will be a wonderful teacher and an advocate for peace.[22]

In Ukraine

The war in Ukraine began with Russia's assault in February 2022. Since the war began, over 41,000 people have died and some 15,000 are missing and, of course, these numbers continue to rise. Millions of people have been displaced, creating a massive refugee crisis, not dissimilar to the refugee

21. Brux, "Yemen Vigil Handout."
22. Alabed, *Dear World.*

crisis caused by the war in Syria. There is a difference though. Ukrainians are white, mostly Christian, and of European heritage, whereas Syrians are people of color, Muslim, and non-European ancestry. Whereas Ukrainian refugees are welcomed throughout the world with open arms, the opposite is the case for Syrian refugees. Yet there are no differences in the humanitarian needs of refugees, regardless of who they are.

Compassionate Encounters. In December 2022, the Ukraine's Children's Choir sang Carol of the Bells in a scheduled performance at New York's Carnegie Hall and an impromptu performance at New York's Grand Central Station. This Christmas carol was written by a Ukrainian musician a century ago. This Christmas, it brought a spirit of joy to those in the audience and to those in the choir. These are the children who practiced while huddling terrified in basements and bomb shelters. They are the ones who were forced to leave their homes for distant locations and were separated from their friends and classmates. And these are the children who are now sharing in a reunion of joy, friendship, hugs, and music, while bringing a message of good tidings to the world.

In the Democratic Republic of Congo (Congo DR)

For decades, the Democratic Republic of Congo has been the scene of one of the world's longest-running conflicts. This central African country is the second-largest country on the continent and is rich in minerals and other natural resources. Indeed, its natural wealth is what has kept the nation a battleground for hundreds of armed groups fighting to control territory and resources, or to use the territory to launch attacks on neighboring countries. At least five million people are internally displaced and one million more are fleeing the country.[23] Along with the armed conflict, the Congolese people are horribly oppressed by militants who kill, maim, rape, and burn down villages.

Compassionate Encounters. "*Your tears are my tears.*" These were the words of Pope Francis in February 2023 when he visited the victims of the Democratic Republic of Congo. The original plan was for him to visit the people in the east of the country where the atrocities were occurring, but high levels of danger and violence kept him at the Vatican Embassy in Kinshasa. The people came to him instead. As he placed his hands on each

---

23. Tsongo, "The Latest Conflict."

person's head or on the stumps that were all that was left of people's arms, he told them,

> To every family that grieves or is displaced by the burning of villages and other war crimes, to the survivors of sexual violence and to every injured child and adult, I say: I am with you; I want to bring you God's caress.[24]

We would call this a compassionate encounter.

In South Sudan

South Sudan is the newest country in Africa, borne of conflict that seems to never come to an end. Around two million people have been forced by fighting and flooding to flee their homes—and women, girls, and little children make up the majority of those displaced. Seventy-five percent of the girls in South Sudan don't go to school, and half of the country's women are married before reaching age eighteen. The country has the world's highest maternal mortality rate, and sexual violence against women and girls is rampant.

Compassionate Encounters. The pope made one more astounding encounter with two religious leaders and with the people of South Sudan. Along with the Archbishop of Canterbury and the Head of the Church of Scotland, Pope Francis was greeted by the people's singing, as is the custom, and he reached out to the victims of oppression. In doing so, he called out especially for women and girls. He pleaded:

> Please, protect, respect, appreciate and honor every woman, every girl, young woman, mother, and grandmother.[25]

This was truly another compassionate encounter in a world where there is far too little compassion and far too many violent encounters.

---

24. Winfield, et al., "Your Tears are My Tears." According to the authors, "the intimate encounter at the Vatican Embassy in Kinshasa was an extraordinary moment of a pastor seeking to console his flock."

25. Winfield, et al., "Pope Pleads for Respect."

QUESTIONS FOR DISCUSSION

1. Were you already familiar with the countries discussed in the chapter? With Yemen? Congo? South Sudan?

2. Were you already familiar with the various groups of people in the chapter? The Rohingya? The Uighurs? The Yazidis? The people of Tigray? The people of Nagorno-Karabakh?

3. Which groups of people or countries do you have the greatest sympathy for?

4. Which of the compassionate encounters affected you most?

5. Do you feel that you care more about struggling and oppressed global populations now that you know more about them?

Knowing The Exploited

Chapter 7

The Exploited In America

CAPITALIST ECONOMIES RELY ON market forces to determine which goods and how many of them are produced, which workers and how many of them are hired, and which land and how much of it is utilized. The market determines the prices of goods, services, labor, and land, as well as the distribution of the goods and services. Producers make decisions based on profits, and unless laws are created and enforced by the government, or unless large numbers of people are involved in consumer, worker, and other organized people's movements, private businesses may have few qualms about exploitation of the labor force, failed consumer protection, environmental harm, and others forms of exploitation. And, to the extent there is market power, which we will consider shortly, this may well translate into political power. We begin by considering the exploitation of labor. Note that the first examples are linked to the meat processing industry and the companies that clean their facilities.

EXPLOITED LABOR

Sweatshop Labor

The term "sweatshop labor" can be used more broadly, but it usually calls forth images of old and dangerous factories where workers experience unsafe conditions. With the onset of the coronavirus pandemic in 2020, many Americans lost their jobs. Many others continued working safely from home, and others worked in industries that were deemed by the government to be "essential." Meat processing was declared essential, and in the context of COVID-19, meat processing workplaces became dangerous "sweatshops". Workers were crowded along assembly lines and were not provided with masks and other protective gear or equipment. Workers in meat processing are disproportionately Black and Hispanic, and they continued working despite the absence of precautions to ensure their safety amidst COVID-19. The failure to assure worker safety in these industries is one of the reasons for the disproportionately high rates of COVID-19 infection and death among Blacks and Hispanics.

Compassionate Encounters. Perhaps it was far too little and far too late, but it was at least some consolation that the House Select Subcommittee on the Coronavirus Crisis published a report in which they revealed the higher death rates among workers in meat packing companies than were previously acknowledged. The report placed the blame on meatpacking companies themselves (though one could also argue that then-President Trump was partly at fault for inappropriately designating meat processing as an essential activity). And, as evident below, capitalism itself was at fault for prioritizing profit maximization. Here is a segment from this report.

> Instead of addressing the clear indications that workers were contracting the coronavirus at alarming rates due to conditions in meatpacking facilities, meatpacking companies prioritized profits and production over worker safety, continuing to employ practices that led to crowded facilities in which the virus spread easily.[1]

Workers began to demand their rights, staging walkouts over their safety concerns. Some plants responded by installing dividers between workstations and slowed their production lines in order to widen the space between workers. A few companies offered financial incentives to keep workers on the job. Others provided safety measures. Tyson, for example, said it spent over $700 million on COVID-19 safety measures and by introducing on-site medical services to its plants. At one point, the company announced that 96 percent of its workers were vaccinated.

Child Labor

In December 2022, news was released that dozens of minors were being injured on overnight shifts at meatpacking plants in Arkansas, Nebraska,

1. Hassan, "Coronavirus Cases and Deaths."

Missouri, and Minnesota. Children as young as thirteen had been hired by Packers Sanitation Services to clean the meatpacking facilities, using chemicals that cause severe burning of the skin and machinery that was large, dangerous, and with razor-sharp edges. It was later revealed that over one hundred children were hired.

The U.S. Fair Labor Standards Act prohibits children from working for more than three hours during school days, overnight, and with hazardous equipment. But the laws protect children only as well as they are followed and enforced.

Industry experts say this scandal is just the 'tip of the iceberg' of America's child labor crisis. Labor officials and experts on child abuse say the number of child laborers may be in the hundreds of thousands. Faced with low unemployment rates and a shortage of adult workers, bosses have turned to teens to fill the gap.

Child labor is not the only problem associated with Packers Sanitation Services. Within the last few years, four workers have allegedly sustained grievous bodily injury resulting in amputation, while another three have died on the job. Neglect of safety procedures was so severe that one of the workers was allegedly beheaded while cleaning slaughterhouse equipment. These examples indicate two issues: sweatshop labor and child labor at Packers Sanitation Services.[2]

Immigrant Child Labor

The children who were discovered cleaning the meatpacking companies were overheard speaking Spanish. Hence, their immigration status was suspect. If indeed they were immigrant children, then they were three types of victims: victims of sweatshop labor, child labor, and exploited immigrant labor. Unscrupulous managers benefit from the influx of desperate young migrants who need cash, and they don't ask questions. Businesses intentionally prey upon the vulnerable immigrant community, both old and young.

Compassionate Encounters. Federal investigators held a midnight visit to a plant where children were suspected of working. They spoke with children as young as thirteen who were operating dangerous machinery. Packers Sanitation Services was subsequently ordered by the government to fire underage workers, to sanction managers who had been involved in

2. Reinl and Patnoe, "Slaughterhouses."

hiring them, and to hire outside consultants to review its hiring policies.[3] The company was fined $1.5 million in penalties for hiring the children.

We are well aware that unaccompanied child immigrants are gravely vulnerable to abuse. The United Nations Children's Organization, UNICEF, published a report stating that a new approach is needed to ensure that unaccompanied migrant and asylum-seeking children in the United States receive proper reception, care and support services. According to this report:

> Each year, thousands of unaccompanied migrant and asylum-seeking children make their way to the U.S., with many fleeing violence and devastating poverty or in the hope of reuniting with family members. These children are brimming with hope and potential, but they are among the most vulnerable in the world.

In a sense, the UNICEF report has become a compassionate encounter, such that the report "provides a roadmap showing how the U.S. government and its partners can draw on experiences in the United States and globally to develop a long-term vision for reception, care and protection of unaccompanied children."[4]

It is comforting that the U.S. judicial system and UNICEF are taking a stand on behalf of unaccompanied migrant children and child workers more generally. Consumers also have a role to play in protecting against capitalist exploitation that includes sweatshop labor, child labor, and exploited immigrant labor. We can demand an end to these practices in letters to the editor and by contacting our legislative representatives. We can speak to business managers and refuse to buy products associated with inequitable labor practices. We can stand with children by speaking out for them, and assuring they are safe and in school. We can come together to support immigrants, guaranteeing they are welcomed and not abused. We can also stand with those whose work is exploited due to their race, ethnicity, or nationality. We can use our tremendous role as consumers to insist that workers are treated justly. What better way for us as consumers to engage in compassionate encounters than to tell retail managers why we will no longer buy any products from their stores!

3. Vondracek, "Child Labor."
4. UNICEF, "Building Bridges."

Exploited Immigrant Adult Labor

Two brothers from an indigenous Oaxacan community in Mexico recently discussed with their wives their plan to go to America, find jobs, and return in a few years with money to better provide for their families. Nine days after they left, one of the wives, Luz Estrella, was breastfeeding her son as the news came on, telling of dozens of Mexicans found dead in an abandoned, sweltering, semi-trailer truck. Her husband had died, and his brother was hospitalized in serious condition. It was one of the deadliest human trafficking tragedies in U.S. history, with 53 victims. Unfortunately, as border crossing becomes more restricted, desperate people become even more desperate. Trump era restrictions still in effect in the summer of 2022 meant that if people were to exercise their internationally guaranteed right to apply for asylum, they would have to enter the United States illegally and then turn themselves over to border agents. They could then file for asylum, and either be released on their own or held in detention while awaiting adjudication of their asylum claims. Sadly, this would not be the case for the two brothers.

Compassionate Encounters. Trump era immigration restrictions are gradually retreating, though Biden policy is not yet clear. What *is* clear is that we need legislation putting just and humane laws into place and clearly publicizing them to all people, including the immigrants themselves. We also need a means of safe transport of desperate migrants to the U.S. Border. In the meanwhile, the church attended by the two wives sent their congregants to visit the women as they mourned one husband and worried about the other. The people bowed their heads as the minister read psalms. The minister said that at the time the husbands left, he felt as though his two arms had been cut off.[5] *His empathy and compassion were evident.*

EXPLOITED BODIES

In the United States, human trafficking and sex trafficking are usually addressed together, as they both involve taking humans and forcing them into some type of activity. We will focus on sex trafficking, which intentionally follows the section on exploited labor because forced sexual relations, and the transport and "sale" or "rental" of human bodies for sex is a profitable business, amounting to billions of dollars for traffickers. Pimps are often

5. Miller, "Brothers' Hope for Work."

part of organized crime rings, and they typically search for young people everywhere: in shopping malls, at high school events, in local clubs, on city streets, in homeless encampments—*and on the Internet!* Youth who are experiencing problems at home or any kind of physical, emotional, or sexual abuse, are especially vulnerable. So too are young people who are forced for various reasons to leave their homes, and unaccompanied minors immigrating to the United States. Traffickers often befriend these young people and create an emotional dependency in the victim. This victim may also be financially dependent upon the pimp, and dependent on the trafficker for food and housing. If the trafficker introduces the victim to drugs, this may create a physical as well as an emotional and financial dependency. And as we know, as long as there is a demand for sex, there will be vulnerable victims. There will continue to be sex trafficking.

Compassionate Encounters. There are many organizations that reach out to victims of trafficking, including the U.S. Catholic Sisters Against Human Trafficking.[6] According to their website, this organization is a collaborative, faith-based national network that offers education, assists survivors, and engages in advocacy on behalf of trafficking victims. The members of the organization can be found giving presentations, raising awareness, and engaging in advocacy at the state and federal level. Their services to victims include the provision of shelter, counseling, spiritual support, job placement, and educational scholarships. Surely their efforts constitute compassionate encounters.

CONSUMERISM AND EXPLOITED CONSUMERS

Before we think about the exploitation of consumers, let's pause to examine the issue of consumerism, or perhaps we should call it over-consumption. Americans expend a lot of time, energy, and anxiety in shopping. They also spend a lot of money. Their children "need" the popular items other children have. They "need" the clothing with the faces of popular children's characters. They "need" the electronic games they see advertised on the Internet. Adults also "need" to be fashionable, and they "need" their homes to be stylish. We "need" to give the nicest gifts, throw the nicest parties, and own the nicest cars, electronics, and large-screen TV's. But do we *really* need these things? Do we *really* need a larger home once our children grow

---

6. Sisters Against Trafficking, http://www.sistersagainsttrafficking.org..

up and move out? Do we really need the boat, the snowmobile, and the cabin up north?

No, we don't. We have trouble differentiating between needs and desires. We succumb to advertising. We fail to think of what could be purchased with the money we spend on ourselves for those with far fewer material goods. Think of what a wonderful world it would be if, rather than spending surplus money on themselves, people with money spent it on the needy. If people without need for gifts gave them instead to the poor. If people with big houses shared them with the homeless, the trafficked, the abused, and the refugee. We know it isn't always that simple, and we know we live within constraints. But by imagining what is possible, we can come closer to achieving it.

The Flint water crisis was a public health emergency that began in 2014 after the drinking water for the city of Flint, Michigan was contaminated with lead and possible Legionella bacteria. Amid a budget crisis, Flint had changed its water source to the Flint River. Residents complained about the taste, smell, and appearance of the water. Officials had failed to apply corrosion inhibitors to the water, which resulted in lead from aging pipes leaching into the water supply, exposing around 100,000 residents to elevated lead levels. A pair of scientific studies confirmed that lead contamination was present in the water supply.

Between 6,000 and 12,000 children were exposed to drinking water with high levels of lead. Children are particularly at risk from the long-term effects of lead poisoning, which can include a reduction in intellectual functioning and an increased chance of future Alzheimer's disease. Furthermore, the water was considered a possible cause of an outbreak of Legionnaires' disease that killed twelve people and affected another 87, but the original source of the bacteria was never found. Ultimately, Michigan's former Governor Rick Snyder and eight other officials were charged with 34 felony counts and seven misdemeanors for their role in the crisis. The victims of the water crisis were awarded a combined settlement of over $600 million, with eighty percent going to the families of children affected by the crisis.

An extensive lead service pipe replacement effort has been underway since 2016. Finally, after $400 million in state and federal spending, Flint has secured a clean water source, distributed filters to all who want them, and laid modern, safe, copper pipes to nearly every home in the city. However, a legacy of distrust remains, to the extent that residents often refuse to drink the tap water.[7]

Compassionate Encounters. In 2018, a federal watchdog called on the Environmental Protection Agency (EPA) to strengthen its oversight of state drinking water systems nationwide and to respond more quickly to public health emergencies like that of Flint. The EPA says it agrees with the inspector general's recommendations and is adopting them "expeditiously." It is too late, however, for the children who were exposed to the toxic water in Flint, and they will bear the risks of negative health effects for years to come. This compassionate encounter came too late for many.

EXPLOITED PEOPLE OF THE LAND

Exploited Farmers

Let's first consider the rural population, which of course includes family farms. The U.S. rural sector is smaller than the urban sector, with just 60 million people (roughly 19 percent of the U.S. population). This is the exact opposite of the situation in many of the world's developing countries, especially in Africa and Asia, where most people and especially most poor people live and work in the rural sector. Nevertheless, approximately 97% of U.S. land area lies in rural counties, so geographically, we can say we are a heavily rural nation. Unfortunately, the rural poverty rate is a relatively high 14.1 percent, in contrast to the national poverty rate of 11.4 percent (and the suburban poverty rate of 9.1 percent). The disproportionately high rural poverty rate is about the same as the poverty rate for our nation's central cities. Regrettably, along with rural poverty comes lack of access to healthcare, a serious problem for the rural population's pregnant, sick, and elderly.

When we think of farmers, we often think of the relatively small, family farmers who work hard to provide the world with food while contributing to the economic vitality of our local communities. These farmers are often the backbone of these communities, and their purchases of livestock feed, seeds, fertilizers, and other inputs, as well as consumer goods, support the local business community. Finally, they and their families fill our schools and churches. This description of family farms is certainly true of *some* farms, but the gap between small family farms and large corporate

7. The Associated Press, "Key Moments in Flint, Michigan's Lead-Tainted Water Crisis."

farms and agribusinesses is huge. Unfortunately, our government agricultural support programs largely benefit the biggest and most profitable farms and agribusinesses, and the smaller farms are left to struggle. Most of our commodity assistance programs provide aid dollars on a *per acre* or *per unit* basis. Thus, the farmers with the most acres in production or the largest number of bushels of output receive the most government assistance. We have to wonder why lower income people and smaller businesses pay taxes to support what are frequently highly profitable agribusinesses. This all means that agricultural policy is complicated. We may wish to see an increase in government support of agriculture, but unless major changes are made in our programs, this will mean very little extra support for smaller local farmers and a lot of additional support for the largest and most profitable farm businesses. We need to change the way our agricultural policy works if we wish to reward those closer to the bottom in size and income.

Compassionate Encounters. Farm Aid is one of many groups that advocate for family farms and fight against corporate agriculture. They seek fair farm prices, encourage consumers to buy locally grown food, promote food security and environmental protection, and work on behalf of minority and women farmers.

Farm Aid concerts were founded by Willie Nelson, John Mellencamp, and Neil Young, and have taken place every year since 1985. The music is intended to reflect our nation's pride in our rural environment, which includes our farms and farmers, natural resources, Indigenous cultures, and a rural way of life. These concerts are a form of compassionate encounters between farmers and their supporters.

Exploited Indigenous People

Native Americans in the United States have the highest poverty rate among all racial and ethnic groups, at 24 percent. This is three times the poverty rate of eight percent for non-Hispanic whites. And as already noted, the Native American home ownership rate is very low (55 percent), in contrast to 74 percent for non-Hispanic whites. The high school dropout rate is over twice that of non-Hispanic whites and the uninsured rate is over three times the white rates. All these circumstances are linked. We've already seen that poverty is associated with poor education and low home ownership rates. Lack of home ownership means an absence of collateral and credit history necessary to borrow money for the upgrade of homes and the purchase of businesses, the transfer of wealth (property) to subsequent generations, and a line of credit to help families get through difficult times of job loss, illness, or other difficult circumstances. Indeed, a major reason for negative outcomes, such as a Native American life expectancy that is eleven years below that of whites, is partly due to a lack of capital—physical capital in the form of houses and human capital in the form of education. In the case of Native Americans, another source of negative outcomes is the historical dispossession of Native American land. Like a lack capital, an absence of land constrains the wealth and wellbeing of people (especially those for whom land is such an important part of their culture and livelihoods).

The Red Lake Nation is owned and occupied by members of the Red Lake Band of Chippewa Indians. It is in northern Minnesota, and the land is heavily wooded with many lakes, swamps, peat bogs, and prairies. This is aboriginal land, but through various treaties and land agreements from 1863 to 1902, the Red Lake Nation gave up much of its land. Red Lake relinquished eleven million acres to the United States in 1863 in what is known as the "Old Crossing Treaty." It gave up another three million acres in what was referred to as the "Act for the Relief and Civilization of the Chippewa." Finally, it ceded up a quarter of a million acres, known as the "Western Townships," to the United State government in 1902. The remaining land was never allotted, meaning that all remaining land is held in common by the members of the Band. By keeping this remaining land intact, the Red Lake heritage and tradition are held in place. Ojibwe is spoken by many residents and there is an archives-library program to preserve tribal records and historical material. Because the land is held in common and because the Tribe has the right to limit who can visit or live on the reservation, few non-members live at Red Lake.

Employment on the reservation is very limited, resulting in high unemployment rates. The Tribal Council is the main employer through its government operations and services. There are also several small businesses, including many operated out of people's homes.[8]

Compassionate Encounters. Nolan grew up on the Red Lake Reservation, a star athlete at Red Lake High School. He now coaches the Red Lake Nation football team. The team averages less than twenty players, and coach Nolan instructs his team not to count players on the opposing team because it would be too discouraging. The Red Lake Nation football team hasn't won a game in years, but the players who never win keep coming

---

8. The Minnesota Indian Affairs Council, http://www.lrl.mn.gov.

back. They keep showing up—for the sake of each other, and for the sake of their coach.

Nolan's patience is remarkable. He doesn't kick players off the team for skipping practices or games. He gives of himself to the kids who are there that day, and then he welcomes those who show up the next day with encouragement to keep coming back. He is called "Uncle Nolan" by players who know him well. His voice is calming, kind, and soft. He finds good things even amidst losses—because other things, like the compassion and kindness of the players, are far more important than a football game loss. He counts the growing maturity of his players as victories.

In the postgame huddle, a player shouts, "We've got a good chance at a win this season!" Teammates yell and high-five as they head back to the locker room. "That's the thing about Red Lake football," says the team captain. "No matter how bad we get beat, there's always hope we'll get a win the next week." Another player comments, "Everyone on the team is my family." Conference coaches voted Nolan Coach of the Year after his team went 0–8 a few seasons ago.[9]

Nevertheless, there is sadness. After the teammates go home, Nolan walks off the field alone. He sits in the end zone, tears streaming down his cheeks. Then he visits the grave site of his son, who died in an ATV wreck at the age of ten. Nolan wears a necklace attached to a pendant he never takes off. It holds a picture of his son. At home after some games, Nolan wonders how he keeps doing it. The answer always comes. "I refuse to give up on them," he says. And they refuse to quit on him.

It is sad to live in poverty. It is sad to be unemployed and uninsured. It is sad to drop out of high school and never own your home. But it is sadder still to lose a child. And for the one who lives with this sadness, the memory of his child lives on as he gives to other children. Bless this man and may he and his team someday win!

Exploited Indigenous Children

We keep learning more and more about Indigenous children and their history of removal from their own homes and families and their placement in boarding schools. These schools were vicious, and many children died. Others were sexually assaulted. They were hungry, cold, and ill. They lost their youth, but they also lost their culture.

---

9. Scoggins, "The Red Lake Nation Football Team Hasn't Won A Game In Years."

How do you lose your culture most effectively? By killing of the language. The children were forbidden from speaking their native language. They were punished, sometimes brutally, for speaking their native tongue. And in this way, native languages sometimes died out or barely hung on.

Compassionate Encounters. Jan was thrilled to learn about a Dakota language course taught at the University of Minnesota. She recalls the privilege of being one woman among a very small group of students who made up the first Dakota language class at the university in the early 1970s. The instructors were two older Dakota women who had both grown up on reservations in South Dakota. Teachers and students spent a year together, creating great learning and great memories. Jan was given the name, "Laughing Woman with the Red Hair." This laughing woman recalls learning so much from the teachers about their current daily lives and their previous lives in the boarding schools. She felt so gifted by her instructors' wisdom. Laughing Woman and her teachers experienced what could only be called a compassionate encounter as they celebrated American Indian Month, and this woman with red hair imagines the thrill it must have been for her Indigenous teachers to be teaching the language they loved.[10]

MARKET POWER AND EXPLOITATION

Economists define market power as the ability of an individual firm (or group of firms) to influence the market price of its product. When a few large firms dominate an industry, and especially if they are willing and able to collaborate, they will likely have market power. Market power may sound reasonable to you and not necessarily problematic, but let's think it through. Imagine a competitive industry such as egg production. Ignoring differences in the type and quality of eggs, there many "small" producers of eggs (and I don't mean the chickens), where "small" in this case means "small relative to the market." One egg producer, even if fairly large, nevertheless produces a miniscule share of the entire supply of eggs. Market prices are determined by market demand and supply, and if this single farmer increases or decreases egg production, it will have a miniscule impact on the entire market supply, and therefore no real influence on market price.

On the other hand, if one firm (farmer) produces most of the eggs in the market, or if a few cooperating farmers produce a large share of total egg production, these few farms are then able to alter total market production

10. Meyer, "The Thrill It Must Have Been."

and thereby influence the market price. If they reduce the market supply, for example, they cause an increase in the market price. Market power means that the one large farm (farmer) or a few cooperating farmers can deliberately restrict output in order to drive up prices, and therefore drive up profits. These profits come at the expense of consumers on the one hand, and to the extent that production is restricted, employment is restricted as well. Income distribution suffers by shifting real income from consumers and workers to firms with market power in the form of higher profits.

Whereas market power is problematic in economic terms, it can also translate into inappropriate political power. Let's consider this. Large and powerful firms may lobby our government for protection of their interests. They also donate money to political campaigns. Outcomes may benefit the businesses, such as reduced regulations, limited antitrust enforcement (government controls on market power), and the imposition of trade restrictions in certain protected industries. All of these may be conducive to even greater market power within these already concentrated industries. Trade restrictions, for example, may effectively limit the competition faced by U.S. firms in concentrated industries, thereby enhancing the market power that already exists in the industry.

Unfortunately, consumers do not have the same level of influence over government policy to the extent that large and powerful business firms do. Consumers are diffuse and unorganized, and don't often see the relationship between market power and higher prices, for example.

Therefore, to the extent that firms in large, profitable, concentrated industries can influence government policies with their financial wealth and power, we do not have a true democracy. Our "one person, one vote" sometimes seems more like "one dollar, one vote." One area where this remains controversial is in global conflicts. President Dwight Eisenhower was the first to refer to the "military-industrial complex" many years ago. In the context of wars in Afghanistan and Iraq, contracts for reconstruction and other activities were given to firms such as Halliburton and Bechtel, companies that had strong ties to the George W. Bush administration. This increased their profitability and left some people wondering whether profits were the real reason for the U.S. invasion of Iraq and our war in Afghanistan. We also must wonder about corporations like Boeing profiting from U.S. bombing support in Yemen, and General Mills, profiting from manufacturing in the illegal Jewish settlements in the Palestinian West Bank. Many human rights organizations, including Jewish Voices for Peace and American Muslims for Palestine have declared a consumer boycott of the products of General Mills.

Compassionate Encounters. Even though it is difficult for consumers to organize into a cohesive unit, *it is not impossible!* Especially with the Internet, it is easy to find out about fair trade products, organic and small farmer products, consumer boycotts, and other types of consumer movements. Joining a consumer boycott is one way we can have our own compassionate encounters with victims of oppression, whether they are Palestinians who have lost their homes or concertgoers paying high prices to Ticket Master, which has been charged with using its market power to the detriment of consumers. As more people learn about Uighur labor in cotton production, or unsafe work conditions in certain factories, or child labor in cleaning companies, we can talk about it, write about it, and then take a stand on it. If enough of us decide not to do business with the offending company, then we *can* make a difference.

QUESTIONS FOR DISCUSSION

1. What is the fundamental reason for the exploitation of labor? Who or what is to blame?

2. Child labor, even if it were not particularly abusive, nevertheless keeps children from attending school. Why is education so important?

3. Have you ever participated in a consumer boycott? What was the effect?

4. Have you ever spoken to the manager of a retail outlet about their sourcing or business practices? How did the conversation go?

5. Many farmers are conservative and do not realize that government policies, such as support prices and trade restrictions, either directly harm the farm sector or primarily benefit large farms and agribusiness. Do you think local farmers understand the need for altering our entire agricultural program structure if we wish to provide greater benefits to them and small farmers throughout the world rather than large and profitable farms and agribusinesses?

6. What did you think of Coach Nolan? Did you find his story touching?

7. Do you think that market power can translate into political power? How so?

Chapter 8

The Exploited In The World

EXPLOITED LABOR

Child Labor

CHILD LABOR, OF COURSE, is not just an American phenomenon. Global capitalism has created opportunities for local and foreign companies to exploit local workers, including children, in the production of goods and services. Children, for example, are often forced to use their small nimble fingers in the carpet industry in parts of Asia and are virtually chained to the weaving looms. Children are often used for begging or selling items amidst traffic in the larger cities in Africa. Kids work in stone quarries, mines, leather tanneries, textile mills, street sales, scavenging, fisheries, and brick laying. Young girls are forced into marriage at a young age. Girls and boys can be bought and sold for the sex trade (as we will see shortly), and boys can be purchased or kidnapped and used as soldiers. Parents are often told that their children will be well-cared for at an attractive place of employment, when in fact they are taken into slavery. These children not only lose their childhood, but they lose the opportunity for education, thereby perpetuating their servitude and passing it down to future generations.

According to the International Labor Organization (ILO) of the United Nations, more than 200 million children in the world today are involved in child labor, doing work that is damaging to their mental, physical, and emotional development. Child labor is typically the result of poverty, and the lack of education for these children only perpetuates their poverty.

Children work because their survival and that of their families depends on it, and it continues to take place even when it is illegal. Sometimes, its very illegality drives it underground, making conditions even worse for children who are working. Almost three quarters of working children are engaged in the worse forms of child labor, including armed conflict, slavery, sexual exploitation, and hazardous work.

In the 1990s, Nike was at the center of a wave of protests after *Life Magazine* reported on the use of child labor in Pakistan. More recently, Hershey was part of a lawsuit that alleged the use of child slaves on cocoa plantations in West Africa. The cosmetics industry sources the mineral mica, which gives their products a sheen, from the mines in India and Madagascar that reportedly use child labor. And these are just a few of many examples.

Africa ranks highest in the share of children working, at twenty percent, or 72 million children. Asia (and the Pacific) ranks second in both these measures—seven percent of all children and 62 million in absolute terms are working in this region. The African and Asian regions together account for almost nine out of every ten child laborers worldwide. But while the number of child workers in the United States is far smaller, the fact that it occurs in this rich and developed country is in some ways even more shameful.

Compassionate Encounters. David L. Parker is a physician and photographer who visited children around the world in their workplaces—the textile factories, stone quarries, garbage dumps, mines, stables, city streets, and rural fields, while taking their pictures. He shares these visits with us in a book of beautiful photos of beautiful children who, unfortunately, are hard at work. The book is called *Before Their Time: The World of Child Labor*, and you will find in it a mixture of sadness and sweetness.[1]

Slave Labor

While there is overlap between child labor and slave labor (children as slaves), we also focus specifically on slave labor because it can involve both children and adults. Slavery conditions have been found in Côte d'Ivoire, Mauritania, Haiti, Pakistan, India, Nepal, Moldova, Benin, Gabon, and Gambia, and in very high numbers in China, Russia, the Democratic Republic of Congo, Bangladesh, and others. This slavery occurs in the

1. Parker, *Before Their Time.*

production of cocoa, palm oil, cotton, and many other products. It occurs due to poverty and ignorance, and of course, due to other people's greed. When people are desperate for income, they respond to offers of work in the hope these offers are legitimate. It is due to desperate circumstances that people accept such job offers. Once on location for work, workers have no money for transportation to leave the site. They may be physically detained. It is also a common practice for business owners to confiscate workers' passports, promising to return them, but then lying and saying they've been lost or stolen.

Earlier in the book, we addressed the oppression of the Uighur population of Xinxiang Province in China. That story was incomplete, for it is also a tale of exploited slave labor. China is the largest cotton producer in the world, with 84 percent of its cotton coming from the Xinjiang region. Detained Uighurs are forced into fields to grow the cotton and into factories to produce it. These cotton and yarn fibers are used extensively in garment-producing countries such as Bangladesh, Cambodia, and Vietnam, as well as in the production of other forms of textiles and home furnishings. Global fashion brands source clothing from Xinjiang directly, and it is estimated that up to one in five cotton products sold across the world is made by forced labor or labor that involves human rights violations. This is occurring on such a scale that it is unimaginable how most of the world's population is either unaware of it or ignoring it. The forced labor system involves the world's largest incarceration of an ethnic or religious minority since the Holocaust.

Slave labor is also a serious problem in the global palm oil industry. A story from the Associated Press describes the plight of a young man as he sobbed into a phone from a Malaysian plantation run by one of the world's largest palm oil companies, FGV Holdings Berhad. The young man said his boss confiscated and then lost his Indonesian passport. Night after night, he was forced to hide from the authorities, sleeping on the jungle floor. His biggest fear was the roaming tigers. All the while, the young man's supervisor demanded he keep working, tending the heavy reddish-orange palm oil fruit that makes its way into the supply chains of food that is purchased by most of us in the United States. The young man isn't alone. There are millions of workers from the poorest corners of Asia working in the palm oil industry in just the two countries of Malaysia and Indonesia alone. The most serious abuses include child labor, outright slavery, and rape. Together, the two countries produce about 85 percent of the world's estimated

$65 billion supply of palm oil. It is almost impossible to avoid purchasing palm oil, as it is labeled as an ingredient under more than 200 different names, and it is on about one-half of all supermarket shelves. It is used in everything from baby formula to candy bars to plywood. We can scarcely avoid buying it.[2]

Compassionate Encounters. Just two weeks after the story of the young man was published, tens of thousands of workers and union leaders joined together in a national strike to protest a new law in Indonesia that further slashes protections for labor and the environment.[3]

Perhaps just as importantly, nonprofit organizations in the United States met together and filed a petition to the U.S. Customs and Border Protection's Office of Trade to address this exploitation. An executive assistant commissioner responded,

> We would urge the U.S. importing community again to do their due diligence. We would also encourage U.S. consumers to ask questions about where their products come from.

The office went further than words and blocked the imports of palm oil from a major Malaysian producer after finding indications of slave labor, child labor, and physical and sexual abuse. They also found that some Rohingya workers had been trafficked onto plantations and forced to work.[4]

Perhaps we think something like this could only happen with "vile, foreign companies," but never American ones. Not true. The Malaysian company responsible for the horrors just mentioned is a joint venture with U.S. Proctor and Gamble. The products flow into the supply chains from FGV and the closely associated Malaysian company Felda, to companies like Nestlé, L'Oréal, and Unilever. They also utilize Western banks and financial companies.

Sweatshop Labor

Garment factories are notorious for their faulty construction and unsafe practices that have resulted in highly publicized incidents resulting in death for their workers. In Bangladesh, for example, safety rules are often violated, especially in industrial settings. As a result, there has been an extraordinary

2. Mason and McDowell, "Palm Oil Labor Abuses."
3. Fardah, "Thousands of Workers Protest New Law."
4. Mason and McDowell, "U.S. Blocks Malaysian Producer's Palm Oil."

number of factory fires since 2005, causing hundreds of deaths. The deadliest single fire occurred in 2012, killing 112 people. More recently in 2021, 52 people were killed in a fire. An even worse accident occurred with the collapse of factories in 2013, when over 1,100 people were killed. Keep in mind these factories produce clothing purchased by U.S. consumers like you and me.

Compassionate Encounters. Green America is a consumers' organization dedicated to reducing sweatshop labor. According to their website,

> Through the purchases you make, and those you choose to avoid, you have the power to create an economy where child labor and sweatshops cease to exist. And your voice, together with the voices of others, can help encourage companies here and abroad to ensure that all workers are paid fairly and treated with respect.[5]

This organization suggests that we do the following:

- Demand sweatshop-free products where we shop.
- Buy union-made, local, and secondhand clothing.
- Buy Fair Trade products.
- Ask questions about sourcing.
- Mobilize at workplaces, schools, and community sites. Sell fair trade products.
- Use your shareholder clout.
- Educate others.

It is fairly easy to use sites such as Green America to identify products that are produced by sweatshop labor and those that are not. Many people are joining with others to spread the word and change consumer behavior. Truly, these efforts by consumers constitute compassionate encounters that can impact the practices of large powerful firms.

5. Green America, http://www.greenamerica.org.

EXPLOITED BODIES

Sex Trafficking

Sex trafficking is, as noted, a specific form of human trafficking, with people falling victim to the sex trade all around the world. There is also overlap between child labor and sex trafficking, as the victims of the sex industry are often children. The relationship between sex trafficking and other social justice issues, such as poverty, is complex.

Sexual trafficking victims come from a range of backgrounds. Some come from economically privileged families, such as some of those we've already considered in the United States. Many others are trying to escape poverty and other forms of oppression. Some live in communities with limited resources and few opportunities for employment. Criminals take advantage of these vulnerable people, offering them a way to escape the harsh realities of their lives. Traffickers may fraudulently offer job training and educational opportunities, but in reality, they offer prostitution to people who are desperate enough to risk everything for a better life for themselves and their families. Traffickers target people who have few economic opportunities and are struggling to meet basic needs. Poor parents, promised that their child will be educated, fed, and treated well, may send their child into slavery. Or parents may feel forced to sell one child so that the others may eat. At times, a child may be sold as payment for a parent's debt (bonded placement), particularly in societies where it is socially acceptable for children to work. Most victims of trafficking are women and girls. In those economically troubled countries where women hold low social status, families may sell a girl child in order to have money to support the rest of the family. Other women and girls are lured into trafficking out of a desire for a better life for themselves, and in some cultures, to pay a dowry.

The number of at-risk people and those suffering from trafficking has increased in the 2020's. This can be explained by the exploitation of vulnerabilities caused by instability due to armed conflicts, other forms of violence, climate change, and economic crises.

Those attempting to flee their homes in hopes of finding safety and employment often find themselves at the mercy of inadequate laws protecting migrants and asylum seekers. They are easily entangled in the webs woven by traffickers. Additionally, traffickers have increased their use of information technology for recruitment and exploitation, luring victims on social media and posting fake jobs on the internet.

Human traffickers often use violence, which includes physical, psychological, and spiritual. People are reduced to objects to be used and exploited for profit.

Compassionate Encounters. The 2023 International Day of Prayer was designated by the U.S. Catholic Sisters Against Human Trafficking to bring awareness of human trafficking. The U.S. Catholic Sisters is the anti-trafficking group that was introduced in the previous chapter. It is a collaborative, faith-based network that provides educational programs and materials, assists survivors with support services, and engages in legislative advocacy. The Catholic sisters believe that becoming educated on the root causes of poverty will help us understand what we can do to decrease global poverty and thus the sex trafficking of human beings.[6]

Vaccine Testing

Two top French doctors said on live television that coronavirus vaccines should be tested on poor Africans, leaving viewers horrified. Nevertheless, this is exactly the outcome that occurred.[7]

The situation of vaccine testing is complicated. Vaccines need to be tested for safety and efficacy in the populations among which they will be used because different people respond differently to vaccines. The African continent is one of vast diversity and vaccines need to be assessed for this population with high levels of co-morbidity, conditions favoring rapid transmissions, and constrained healthcare opportunities. At the same time, it is essential that ethical practices be adopted. Among these are informed consent, detailed explanations of side effects, and the option to withdraw from the study.

Some fear, however, that trial enrollment practices target the poor as guinea pigs. Unfortunately, this has happened before. For example, during a meningitis outbreak, children were enrolled without parental consent in a 1997 trial in Nigeria that caused eleven deaths and other permanent disabilities. These types of tragedies leave people worried that foreign nations view Africa as a testing ground. Furthermore, trials must be followed by ethical distribution of vaccines. This has not been the case for COVID-19, as wealthier countries were first to receive large numbers of the vaccine. The

6. U.S. Catholic Sisters Against Human Trafficking, "International Day of Prayer." www.sistersagainsttrafficking.org.

7. Kossoff, "Coronavirus Vaccines."

paradigm of testing in lower-income countries for the benefit of wealthier nations is one to be avoided.

The most obvious question is this: Are poor people driven by their poverty to participate in a study in which they would not otherwise participate if there was no need for financial payoff? If so, their participation is not entirely voluntary. Challenges remain, but so too does the need for widespread, ethical, African participation in the quest for equitable vaccine access.[8]

Compassionate Encounters. The encounters that occurred were not very compassionate, though they *were* anti-racist. And the encounters were not in person but were virtual via Twitter. One person from Côte d'Ivoire tweeted, "It is totally inconceivable we keep on cautioning this. Africa isn't a testing lab. I would like to vividly denounce those demeaning, false and most of all deeply racist words." Someone from Senegal tweeted, "Welcome to the West, where white people believe themselves to be so superior that racism and debility become commonplace. Time to rise."[9] More importantly, it is time for those of us in the richer countries to come together to determine how to make vaccine testing truly voluntary.

Unexploded Bombs

This is a news release from Syria Relief Services.

> It is with great sadness that Syria Relief must announce that a 6-year-old boy was killed by an Unexploded Ordnance (UXO) in Sarmin, Idlib on Thursday 31st December. Syria Relief, which operates the school that the child attended and is 400 meters away from where the UXO was found, believes that the initial attack that caused the UXO was from a cluster munition attack on New Year's Day, January 1st, 2020, 364 days earlier.[10]

Furthermore, Syria Relief believes the child, six-year-old Ghaith, was searching for firewood with his four-year-old sister and five-year-old cousin after school hours when he came across an unusual object which he believed to be a toy. He attempted to bring it home, but it exploded in his hands. Despite efforts to save him, he died later in hospital. His sister and

---

8. Boms, et al., "A Case For More Vaccine Trials."

9. Boms, et al., "A Case For More Vaccine Trials."

10. Syrian Relief, Jan 2, 2021. http://www.reliefweb.

cousin were not critically injured and were treated in hospitals locally. Syria Relief's Chief Executive says:

> Despite best efforts to save him, little Ghaith passed away in hospital later on, on New Year's Eve 2020. Such a tragic end to a year with such a tragic start. Cluster munition attacks, aimed at civilians, aimed at children, still have the power to kill one year on. To the sweet, innocent mind of a six-year-old boy, gathering firewood after school to keep his family warm in the winter months, he had no idea he had found a bomb. A bomb which was dropped on a school. *A six-year-old has such a vast imagination, but he could not have possibly imagined that this device was dropped with the intent of killing him and children like him.*[11]

Compassionate Encounters. There is not much that people of the world can do for little Ghaith at this point, but they can help his friends and siblings. Syria Relief is visiting the children of Syria in their schools and communities to teach them about explosives, because unfortunately, they need to learn how to avoid being blown up. They add their prayers, "All of the prayers of the Syria Relief team are with Ghaith, his family, the community in Sarmin and we hope that in the year 2021 we no longer have to announce the death of a child killed in Syria, which has become heartbreakingly common for us over the ten years of the Syrian conflict."[12] The compassion of Syria Relief is evident.

EXPLOITED PRODUCERS

Economists often implicitly assume the existence of competitive markets, even though competitive markets are rarely the case. This is especially true in developing countries, where there may be several impediments to free markets. Market power can exist in many fashions.

A good example is the coffee market. Farmers in remote villages in Ethiopia grow what may be the best coffee beans in the world, but if their only option is to sell them is to a single buyer who periodically visits the villages, they will be forced to accept any very low price that is offered to them for their beans. They have no alternative, since the absence of multiple buyers prevents competition among them, which would in turn drive up prices for the growers. The buyer pays little, and then ships the coffee

11. Syrian Relief, http://www.reliefweb.
12. Syrian Relief, http://www.reliefweb.

beans to agribusinesses in the United States and elsewhere, where they are packaged, marketed, and sold at high prices due to the market power that exists in the larger coffee industry. This coffee industry is highly concentrated, resulting in high prices paid to the coffee-related companies despite the low prices paid for the coffee beans themselves. In other words, there is market power on behalf of both the coffee bean buyer (technically called monopsony when there is just one buyer of the unprocessed agricultural product) and on the part of the agribusinesses that process the beans and sell the coffee. As a result, the consumer pays a high price for coffee, while the impoverished grower receives next to nothing. One response has been for farmers to destroy their coffee bean crops and convert their land to the production of khat (a plant-based drug that is popular in East Africa and Arabia as a stimulant.) The common assumption that free and competitive trade always takes place is far from the truth.

Compassionate Encounters. In 1946, a woman named Edna Ruth Byler visited women in a sewing class in Puerto Rico to examine their needlecrafts. She discovered the women had a talent for creating beautiful lace, but she also realized that the women lived in extreme poverty despite their hard work. They had very few buyers for their lace and were therefore paid very low prices for it. Byler began carrying these lace pieces back home to the United States to sell at relatively high prices. She then returned the money to the groups of women creating them. This laid the groundwork for the first Fair Trade organization, the Mennonite Central Committee. Since then, the fair-trade movement has taken off and fair-trade products are widely available in the United States today. These include products like coffee, tea, chocolate, textiles, and many others.

You and I play an important part in our role as consumers of internationally produced products. When we buy products that are certified as fair trade, we are assured that the producers of the products receive fair prices. This often works through farmer-owned cooperatives; and by cutting out many of the "middlemen" and the profits of the major corporations, consumers can buy a superior product at a reasonable price and know that the benefits of the sale will accrue to the poor farmer and his or her village.

The same holds true of our role as consumers of other products that may have been sourced by companies using child labor, slave labor, and sweatshop labor. There is so much we can do as compassionate shoppers! First, we can educate ourselves by searching the Internet for organizations that address these topics (search for "fair trade") One example is the

Anti-Slavery International.[13] Second, we can speak with the managers of retail outlets where we buy our clothing and other products. We can tell them we are very concerned about the exploitation of labor and would like to know where and how their products are sourced. You might be surprised to learn that some large retailers play a positive role in assuring safe working conditions for their product sources. If you learn otherwise, you can stop shopping at that store and explain your reasons to the manager. Or, if you want to make a larger difference, you can gather with friends in schools, churches, and other organizations and organize a boycott of the offending products, or search for a boycott already underway on the Internet. Lastly, you and your friends can sell fair trade products through your church or other organizations and encourage local businesses to sell fair trade products as well. Our buying decisions may indeed affect the practices of international companies, and our roles as compassionate consumers can translate into compassionate encounters.

EXPLOITED FARMERS

The U.S. government subsidizes American farmers and agribusinesses, enabling and encouraging them to produce large amounts of farm products, such as wheat, rice, corn, tobacco, and cotton. When these large supplies of agricultural products enter world markets, they force down global market prices, to the detriment of small and often poor farmers in developing countries. Cotton is a case in point. It is a crop that can be produced relatively cheaply in countries such as India, where land and farm labor are cheaper than in the United States. Yet, despite their cost advantage, farmers in India cannot compete with U.S. farmers and agribusinesses that sell their products at low prices that are nevertheless profitable due to the generous subsidies of the U.S. government. Similarly, these small Indian farmers pay high prices for their inputs due to market power on behalf of the agribusinesses that make and distribute them. India's farmers become poorer, due to the combination of low prices for their products but high prices for their inputs. In some cases, they become desperate. Indian farmers literally drink their pesticides, which are widely publicized as "cotton suicides."

Compassionate Encounters. Two researchers went to India to study the situation. They found that an average of 48 farmers committed suicide per day in India between 1995 and 2018. They were told the stories of cotton

13. Anti-Slavery International, www.antislavery.org.

suicides by surviving families. They learned that by going into debt, farmers were entering a long-term tradition connected with webs of families and castes that creates a profound sense of humiliation and hopelessness. Suicide resolves the farmers' humiliation.[14] The work of these researchers is essential if the world is to understand the underlying causes of the cotton suicides and seek to change them. The circumstances are dictated by a complex web of tradition in India and market power in the developed world. Educating the global population is the first step in a compassionate encounter.

AN EXPLOITED PLANET

The impacts of climate change include changing weather patterns, rising sea levels, and extreme weather events. Such events have increased in frequency and severity, and include hurricanes, tornados, floods, wildfires, droughts, and periods of extreme heat. They impact food production, resource availability, people's livelihoods, violent conflict over resources, and migration. They are especially tragic for the poor, the refugee, the pregnant woman, and the child.

Extreme weather events devastate poor people in rich countries like the United States. They cannot easily escape disasters. They lack heating in the frigid cold and air conditioners in grueling heat waves. They cannot afford lost livelihoods, or the spiraling prices of necessities arising from scarcity. They are overwhelmed by the loss of lives, clean water, electricity, and healthcare.

Poor people in poor countries are especially vulnerable to extreme climate events. In agricultural areas, food production is threatened; and in urban areas, livelihoods are undermined. The prices of food, energy, and water spiral. All these are evidenced by recent flooding in Nepal, Indonesia, and Pakistan; cyclones in Zimbabwe and Mozambique; food scarcity in Niger and Uganda; and the destruction of homes and crops in small coastal and island countries like Bangladesh and Timor-Leste. Extreme heat kills the poor in India and other locations when the poor must keep working.

Climate change creates millions of refugees. These include residents of coastal areas as sea levels rise, farmers who lose livelihoods and sustenance during a drought, and people fleeing conflict zones precipitated by resource

---

14. Kannuri and Jadhav, "Cultivating Distress."

scarcity that arises from a warming planet. Ignored by much of the world, these refugees are among the world's most vulnerable.

Children are also especially at risk. A child's developing body is most susceptible to the poisons of smog and the smoke caused by fires. Little children cannot swim amid flooding. Most of all, children suffer the malnourishment that is spreading across the globe as the greatest health consequence of climate change.

Compassionate Encounters. Imagine we could visit the future, a compassionate encounter of sorts with our planet in the days to come. We might find some peace, and we might find contentment. We may find a spirit of kindness and generosity. We might be very happy there. But we will always look back, knowing what we lost.

DEAR FUTURE,

No doubt we were a Dark Ages to you.
And paradoxically we had so much —
for instance the millions of species
we let go extinct on our watch. Our
ignorance, not least of our own wealth, was
inexcusable. Even the land mass
we inhabited was luxurious compared
with your deserts and reduced shorelines.
We enjoyed the relative security
of fixed national boundaries before
irresistible mass climigration
rendered those borders irrelevant.
We fought over things we shouldn't have —
who loved who, how we identified, what we
thought about God—while letting the super-
rich rob us to the last penny. Worst, though,
was our willingness to let distractions
prevent our seeing the real damage
our way of life was doing to the planet
as a habitat hospitable to our
species, not to mention those countless
other species to whom Earth belonged.
For that alone I fear our age will live
in infamy as long as sentient beings

dwell in the house of the universe. dwell in the house of the universe.
[. . .]

> We have to imagine that there is still hope, that someone some-
> where will pick up an envelope, and have the grace to build our
> planet for a better future.

[. . .] Dear future, I know you're an abstraction,
that I'm in fact writing not to our imagined
descendants but to us here, now.
Indeed, we are the ones who need to read
this letter, not you, because without our
contrite and dedicated action,
there may be no "you." So I fold the pages
of my hope and grief into this envelope
and let it fall to the ground before reaching
a mailbox, on the chance that another
may pick it up, open it, read it, and
join with us in changing the present,

Thomas R. Smith[15]

WHAT CAN WE DO?

We've already gotten a head start, for we cannot care about people we know nothing about. So, we begin by learning about the world's discarded and exploited people and our exploited planet. Next, we can tell others about them. And then we can act!

Bread for the World is a national Christian citizens' lobby for issues of world and domestic hunger and poverty. It began in the early 1970s amidst the world hunger crisis, and your author was one of the first members. Indeed, she decided to earn her Ph.D. in economics in order to learn whether the policy proposals of Bread for the World were indeed valid. (They are.) Bread for the World educates people with their website and handouts. (www.bread.org). They visit the offices of legislators and encourage their support for appropriate legislation. They provide us with the information we need to know about pending legislation. And perhaps most importantly, they encourage us to contact our legislators in support of appropriate legislation.

---

15. Smith, "Dear Future."

It is easy to feel hopeless—one, because there are so many suffering people; and two, because we are each only one person. But through organizations like Bread for the World, our voices are magnified, and our efforts can make a real difference.

And, we can be kind amidst compassionate encounters. What we do for one person can mean the world to them. We can also contact the various organizations that address homelessness, criminal justice, and others to see how we might help. We can lead a movement or join a movement for Fair Trade products, transparent cotton sourcing, sustainable production, and other issues involving consumers, producers, workers, and the environment. We can talk to store managers. We can start Fair Trade sales. We can boycott stores and companies and even states and countries that are known to treat people badly. We can educate others. We can put together our collective heads and undoubtedly come up with so much more. We *can* make a difference!

QUESTIONS FOR DISCUSSION

1. There were several individual people mentioned in this chapter. Were there any for whom you felt greater compassion?

2. Is there anything you can do to assist this person or people in similar situations?

3. Does your school, church, or place of employment offer fair trade products for sale? Can you and others sign a petition requesting the sale of fair-trade products?

4. Does your community have stores that sell fair trade products? Would you like to speak with business managers or owners and ask if they would include fair trade products on their shelves?

Where Do We Go From Here?

Chapter 9

Whose Truth is the Real Truth?

No Truth, No Justice . . . No Justice, No Peace

WHOSE TRUTH IS THE real truth?

America is a nation divided. Child against parent. Friend against friend. Parishioner against parishioner. Americans against each other and those who live in the world beyond. We disagree on the most basic of facts. The outcome of elections. The presence of electoral fraud. The benefits of a vaccine. This conspiracy theory and that one. We cannot heal unless the truth is told. We cannot move on until we face the facts. But whose facts are the real facts? So, we ask, for one last time, "Whose truth is the real truth?"

And now we have to stop all this. Take a pause. Look around. What do we see?

We see that we are all in so much pain. And as animals circle around the wounded creatures of their pride; we must circle around our wounded nation because that is who we are. We care for our wounded.

And wounded we are. Some, like me, feel crushed by the depth of hostility towards people I love. Others feel disregarded and disrespected by a smug elite that has never had their back. Some feel the values they've held forever are now under attack. Still others feel the pain of assault when their precious diversity is blamed for the unhappiness of others. All this pain is real; and that is where the truth-telling begins.

We cannot move on without a truth-telling. Our feelings are tender, made fragile by the harshness of our world today. Our spirits are damaged and our sensitivities raw. *We are a broken people, and if there is one truth we can tell with certainty, it is the truth of our pain.*

Truth-telling was essential for the healing of South Africa in the waning days of apartheid. It was vital in post-genocidal Rwanda, and crucial for a post-Holocaust world. Truth-telling *compels* us to come to grips with America's history of genocide and slavery, its racism, and its contempt for the poor, the immigrant, the person of color, and the person we think is "below us".

As Pope Francis explains, "Truth . . . is an inseparable companion of justice and mercy. All three together are essential to building peace."[1]

So, in the hope of finding justice, mercy, and peace, I will tell you of my truth, if you will tell me of yours. But you should know that until now, I've tried to write in a "dispassionate voice" (i.e., objectively—just the facts and not the feelings). That changes now, as I'm deliberately making this personal.

Here is my truth: My heart hurts for refugees—those who flee the horrific violence and poverty I have seen in the world with my own eyes. The boy afraid of the tiger. The woman afraid of the night. The Somalian refugees I met in a Kenyan camp as they prepared to depart for America— desperate people who fled brutal warlords and terrorists, now excited and trusting and hopeful for a new life in the United States. I welcomed them as my new neighbors across the broader Twin Cities metro as they prepared to journey to Minneapolis and St. Paul.

Traveling many times to Africa, I've been treated with such great respect and kindness. This is a common experience of white people; and some Africans, in turn, are naïve enough to believe that Black Africans traveling to white America will be treated with the same kindness and respect. So, why are they met with such contempt?

In October 2019, a disgraced president held a rally in Minneapolis and railed against the Somali community, calling them a "disaster" from 'f*****g Somalia.'" The worst part: crowds of white people shouted approval for the shameful words of this president. They cheered for him, and they booed the Somalis. They did this in front of their children, before our nation, and for the entire world to see. This is when my heart, already hurting for refugees, finally broke.

Somali women took care of me during a prolonged illness in the Twin Cities hospitals. Somali men transported me gently through the MSP

---

1. Pope Francis, *Fratelli Tutti*, 227.

airport in a wheelchair and spoke with me kindly. Somali parents trusted their young people to me as students in my classroom. And after the former president's rally, they hung their heads and said, "I didn't know we were hated like that."[2]

"Go back to where you came from," they were told after the president said they were dangerous. The president, whose rallies meant, "It is okay to say, 'I hate you' out loud." As hate crimes spiral upward, the Somali community again fears for its safety. I am so sad for these people I care about.

This is my truth, the truth of my pain. It is not my only pain. Living so close to Minneapolis, my heart hurts for George Floyd, killed by a white cop kneeling on his neck while he cried, "I can't breathe." I thought I heard him calling for his mother, and like moms everywhere, I looked back to see if he might be calling for me. And it isn't just George Floyd, but an entire history of Blacks killed by cops in the Twin Cities metro. *Say their names:* Terrance Franklin, Jamar Clark, Philando Castille, Dolal Idd, Daunte Wright, Leneal Lamont Frazier, Amir Locke, Winston Boogie Smith Jr. . . . And how many more? *Say their names.*

HAND IN POCKET
I.M. GEORGE FLOYD

Remember Orwell's picture of the future
in *1984*? *Imagine a boot*
stamping on a human face forever.

Do Black people see in the footage
of Chauvin and Floyd *a White knee*
crushing a Black windpipe forever?

The Black man's neck and shoulder are summer-
bare under the White cop's clothed knee. That should
tell you all you need to know about power.

Somehow almost worse is the cop's leisurely hand
in pocket. Why should that detail disturb us
so? As though the cop were doing nothing

2. Mahamud and Van Berkel, "I Didn't Know We Were Hated."

more than rummaging for car keys. Floyd's
face is contorted while the cop retains
a flat, dispassionate composure. Murder

most casual . . . The Black man, soon to die, calling
for his mother, his cries for life and breath not enough
to roll the stone from the White cop's eyes.

Thomas R. Smith[3]

Minneapolis once belonged to a musician named Prince—a Black man and a purple man who wrote a song about Baltimore and a man named Freddie Gray. Ironically, Prince stopped breathing almost four years to the day before George Floyd took his last breath. The world turned purple, and the capitalists assembled a Prince paraphernalia shop at the Twin Cities MSP airport. Then the world turned black, and they wrote down lives that matter on the signs they carried in the streets. I painted my sign and carried it in the streets.

George Floyd's death under the knee of a white cop in May 2020 impassioned the Black Lives Matter movement, not just in the United States, but across the globe, including Australia, Japan, France, Germany, Kazakhstan, Indonesia, and over sixty other countries. Perhaps most touching are the Black Lives Matter campaigns in Cape Town, South Africa, where the effects of apartheid linger far beyond its official end in 1994, and in Recife, Brazil, where the death of a Black child brought masses of protesters to the streets.

The Twin Cities isn't unique in America. Ten days ago, as I write this, a 32-year-old unarmed Black man named Tyre Nichols was savagely beaten by five Memphis cops as he cried in pain and called for his mother. And like all those other mothers, I again turned back to see if he was calling for me. Like Tyre's mother, I cannot watch the video of his assault. Tyre died three days later. To Tyre's mother, *I am so sorry.*

When does it end? Tonight, I read of another awful incident. A 28-year-old mentally ill Kenyan immigrant described as "deeply loved," "well-regarded," and an "aspiring musician" was allegedly smothered by seven deputies and three hospital employees. Irvo Otieno was handcuffed, shackled, and like George Floyd, had the life snuffed out of him over the twelve agonizing minutes he was forcefully pinned to the ground. His

3. Smith, "Hand in Pocket, i.m. George Floyd."

mother cried. She said, "There is goodness in his music and that's all I'm left with now." Her broken heart was written all over her face in the photo that accompanied the story. I kissed her face. Kenya—home of my African in-laws, where I slept with my daughter-in-law in her only bed, and we cooked and cleaned and swept, and we celebrated Christmas with a roasted goat and a call to prayer from the Imam in the background—*I'm so sorry, Irvo, that America treated you this way.*

Around the country, there were so many more. Freddie Gray and Breonna Taylor. Alton Sterling and Atatiana Jefferson. Some, like George Floyd, couldn't breathe: Eric Garner, Herman Whitfield, Elijah McClain. *Say their names.*

Elijah McClain was a boy I loved—not really a boy, but youthful in his nature. He was respectful, thoughtful . . . He wore a ski mask to stay warm, and he bowed his head to avoid frightening people with the mask. He taught himself to play the guitar and violin, and on his lunch breaks, he played for the abandoned creatures at the animal shelters, believing that music brought them comfort. He refused to kill flies and he didn't eat meat. To the police officers, he said, "You are beautiful and I love you." And the officers killed him. Elijah McClain was a boy I loved. *Say his name.*

This is the truth, the truth of my pain. I hurt for Blacks who fear the police, especially the gentle boy-men like Elijah. I ache for Somalis who fear white racism. My heart hurts for the American poor, treated with contempt, blamed for their poverty, and denied the benefits that ought not be denied in a rich nation like ours. I am especially sad for poor mothers as I look back and wonder how a man like Ronald Reagan is admired today after calling them "Welfare Queens" and "Welfare Cheats" and saying they were lazy. And I look back and wonder how a man like Bill Clinton "ended welfare as we know it" by creating a welfare program that presumed "non-working" women were lazy and needed to be forced "to work," And I think of all the Republicans who ended coronavirus relief because it was "discouraging work" among those women who were so, so lazy. Never mind that their jobs became dangerous. Or that they lost childcare for their kids and residential care for their aging parents. Or that their kids needed their help with virtual learning. Or that, as usual, they cleaned, cooked, swept, shopped for groceries, cooked the meals, did the laundry, and washed the dishes.

I am hurt when honorable people are treated dishonorably. The disgraced former President and his disgraceful friends have made a pass time of this, treating people I care about with ridicule and derision. And today as I write this, the woman who is my heroine announced she will not run again for New Zealand's highest office, and I'm furious that Tucker Carlson referred to Jacinda Ardern 'the lady with the big teeth'.[4] I'm saddened as well that within hours of her announcement, a magazine article featured her "best looks" and "fashion moments."

I cry over photos of dead migrant children washed onto the shores of the Mediterranean and the Rio Grande. I kiss their photos and I hold them to my heart. I am sad for those with empty stomachs—children searching garbage dumps, infants dying before ever living, mothers weeping when yet another baby dies. I speak to the television and tell them I am sorry. I whisper "thank you" to the ones on TV who try to ease their pain.

I sat with women in their dark hot hovels in the slums of Nairobi and I told them I admired their embroidery. I watched as women walked to Kampala to receive free t-shirts in exchange for votes for a Ugandan president and I told them I admired their t-shirts.[5] I sat with village women in Ouagadougou, talking of sex and babies that died; and I dined with shanty-town women in a soup kitchen in Santiago, talking of oral rehydration and babies that survived. I stood in Mexico City's Zócalo on the very spot where generations of protesters stood before me, and I sat in Bamako's airport where young men with big guns stood before me too. I crawled through tunnels made by the Viet Kong half a century ago, and I defied my own rule about donating to reliable charities rather than beggars when I came upon an emaciated Vietnamese woman and her severely malnourished baby. I gave her all the money I had.

It was never all bad. I bought food from old women on Moscow's subway stops, and I watched as babushkas swept the public square outside the Kremlin walls. I visited Gorky Park and its horrible latrines, and I walked through Novodevichy Cemetery, marveling at the graves of Chekhov, Gogol, and Solzhenitsyn. I walked the streets of Legon, Ghana, seemingly alongside the Black diaspora walking the very same streets. And I walked along Cuba's Malecón, mesmerized by cars named Oldsmobile 88, Ford Super Deluxe, Buick Super, and Mercury Monterrey. In Havana, I slept in a

---

4. Bickerton, "The 'Lady With the Big Teeth.'"
5. The Ugandan president is Yoweri Museveni.

bed in which Earnest Hemingway slept. In Cancún, I slept in a bed with a sign that said, "safe, clean room for $5.00 per night."[6]

I danced all night in Mexican dance clubs until I was told they discriminated against Indigenous people. I danced through the night with Ghanaian waiters after my friends went home to bed. I danced until morning in a Russian dance club, all the while saying *spaSEEbah*—thank you—to the guy next to me when I went back and forth from the dance floor.[7] (Poor guy—it turns out he was British.) I danced with Cuban women in their unbecoming but omnipresent spandex. And I'm so very sorry to tell you this, but I sang "Love Me Tender" by Elvis in a Hong Kong Karaoke bar.

Some of these memories are joyful. Sometimes I paint them. I have paintings all over my house of women sweeping floors and huts and courtyards. I do this because it makes me feel a little bit closer to them.

Other memories hurt. It hurts when victims of mental illness are terrorized by what is imagined as much as if the imagined were real. The imaginary tiger is every bit as horrible as the real one. My own heart aches for the broken hearts of mothers whose sons scream at night in fear of the imagined tiger. Sometimes the mothers scream as well. I know—I am one of those mothers.

But most of all—I am haunted by the boy in the real jungle, terrified of the real tigers, reaching his arm out desperately for someone to save him. I painted a picture of this boy, crouching in the jungle, near the tiger. I painted it over and over, as if perfection could somehow save him. I know that it didn't.

As I write these closing words, it is Christmas Eve, 2022. My thoughts turn to shivering children and exhausted mothers arriving at the southern border expecting U.S. Title 42 to be lifted, but one group of politicians asked the Supreme Court not to lift the COVID-19-era ban that denied their entry, and the leader of the other political party asked the Court to lift the ban, but to wait until *after* Christmas. My dreams tonight will mingle with these children and mothers, cold and hungry, perhaps not at all unlike the child and his mother on that first Christmas eve.[8]

---

6. To the reader: Please do not act so frivolously with your safety in Cancún, or anywhere in Mexico, since the U.S. State Department is warning Americans about extensive gang activity and adulterated drugs and medicines and advising us not to go at this time. The same goes for dancing and taking risks in any place away from home.

7. Спасибо in Russian.

8. I wrote this chapter over a period of weeks, where every day seemed important in some way.

COMPASSIONATE ENCOUNTERS

I am healed by my compassionate encounters. My friends and I protest when migrants are mistreated, when another unarmed Black man is killed by the police, and when metro mosques are attacked by arsonists. We first came together to protest the Iraqi invasion, which took place exactly twenty years ago today as I write this. Since then, we've learned the art of persuasion, we've nourished each other with potlucks, and we've never, ever stopped believing in what is just. My American friend wrote the poems in this book. My Palestinian friend joined me to memorialize the murdered journalist Shireen Abu Akleh. My dear Iranian friend, Hossein, met with me to mourn the death of Mahsa Amini. My other women friends voted for Hossein to be an honorary woman so we could all stand together as one in support of protesting Iranian women. We all stuck together through the mixture of cheers and hate ("I hope you all burn in hell, you communists"). We survived the blizzards and summer heatwaves. We experienced COVID-19 and strokes and deaths and loss.

Each day finds more compassionate encounters. I smiled as I read of kindergarten children together in half-day English and half-day Somali immersion classes. I was delighted when I just discovered that the photographer for *Before Their Time: The World of Child Labor* is my neighbor in the Twin Cities metro.[9] And I grin in the morning when I sweep the floor, feeling "one with the women of the world," despite my privilege, in this one simple way, whether we are sweeping huts or yards or plain old floors like mine.[10]

WHAT IS THE TRUTH OF YOUR PAIN?

And what is the truth of your pain?

Do you work without joy, care for children without means, and make no headway despite your backbreaking labor?

---

9. Parker, *Before Their Time*.

10. I am well aware of my privilege. And perhaps I am not worthy of writing intimately about people I don't really know. Tyre, Elijah, Irvo, the drowned children along the seashore, the boy in the jungle . . . But I think about them a lot and I imagine their suffering. I am terribly sad for their mothers and fathers. I can only hope their families and communities will allow me to ally with them in this way, and if not, they will forgive my presumptuousness.

Are you lonely in a culture that abandoned you in your homelessness, your mental illness, or your nursing home? Or maybe just your living room or your bottle of wine?

Are you frightened, overwhelmed, traumatized, and pushed out of the way to make room for the privileged? Is each day another kick in the face and a gut punch to the stomach? Are you shamed for your ignorance, ignored by the better-off, and forgotten by your chosen leader?

Or are you one who is privileged, yet misunderstood, unloved, presumed to be snobbish, and hurt by those whose words are cruel?

There are a million types of pain, and a million people suffering. Humanity bears a terrible burden of hurt. But rather than turning our hurt to hate, we can acknowledge our pain and the pain of others. Then we can engage in compassionate encounters to try to heal that pain.

QUESTIONS FOR DISCUSSION

1. What is the truth of your pain?

2. Have you been helped by compassionate encounters? Please explain.

3. With which group do you most closely identify? The populist's base of support? The elite establishment? The scapegoats? If you chose the latter, how are you scapegoated?

4. Which of the discarded and exploited people causes your greatest pain? Why is this the case?

5. How can you engage in a compassionate encounter with those you've identified in question #4?

Chapter 10

Conclusions

THE STORY OF A VISIT

Just as both the Saint and the Pope with the mutual name of Francis had inspirational visits with important Muslim leaders, this white Catholic woman had her own compassionate encounter with an important Muslim leader—the Director of the Minnesota chapter of CAIR (the Council on American Islamic Relations). On a snowy winter's eve in December 2022, as the thoughts of many turned to Christmas, Hanukkah, and Kwanzaa, and the hearts of many others looked forward to Eid al-Adha and Eid al-Fitr, CAIR held a celebration for its supporters.[1] Jaylani Hussein, Director of the organization, shared a visit with me that was full of kindness and warmth. I gave Jaylani a picture I had painted of the beautiful Masjid An-Nur, the Minneapolis Mosque of the Light, because a magnificent blue dome of beauty can truly bring light to us all.

THE GOOD SAMARITAN

Pope Francis tells the story of one more compassionate encounter, that of the Good Samaritan. This was the person in the Bible who stopped along a road to care for a stranger who needed help. The pope's purpose is to show

---

1. CAIR-MN works to enhance the understanding of Islam, encourage dialogue, protect civil liberties, empower American Muslims, and build coalitions that promote justice and mutual understanding. It advocates for the civil rights of Muslims and other racial, religious, and ethnic minorities facing discrimination.

that "the existence of each and every individual is deeply tied to that of others."[2] He explains in more detail:

> The parable eloquently presents the basic decision we need to make in order to rebuild our wounded world. In the face of so much pain and suffering, our only course is to imitate the Good Samaritan.[3]

The pope continues:

> The parable . . . speaks to us of an essential and often forgotten aspect of our common humanity: we were created for fulfilment that can only be found in love. We cannot be indifferent to suffering.[4]

When examining the characters in this Gospel story—the stranger, the Good Samaritan, and the various people who just walked by—the pope makes a startling pronouncement: there are only two kinds of people in the story—those who stop and help, and those who go on their way. There are only two kinds of people in this world: those who stop and those who go on.

Two kinds of people? Not Democrats and Republicans? Not populists and progressives? Nationalists and globalists? Believers in one ideology or another? No—it isn't the ideology that matters here, especially to the needy stranger. The pope explains:

> the decision to include or exclude those lying wounded along the roadside can serve as a criterion for judging every economic, political, social and religious project . . . [All other] distinctions, labels and masks fall away: it is the moment of truth. Will we bend down to touch and heal the wounds of others? Will we bend down and help another to get up?[5]

Not only is ideology irrelevant in this sense, but to a degree, so is religion. The two people who walked past the needy stranger were religious—a Levite and a priest. According to Pope Francis, this shows:

> that belief in God and the worship of God are not enough to ensure that we are actually living in a way pleasing to God. A believer may be untrue to everything that his faith demands of him, and

2. Pope Francis, *Fratelli Tutti*, 66
3. Pope Francis, *Fratelli Tutti*, 67
4. Pope Francis, *Fratelli Tutti*, 67.
5. Pope Francis, *Fratelli Tutti*, 70.

yet think he is close to God and better than others. . . . Paradoxically, those who claim to be unbelievers can sometimes put God's will into practice better than believers.[6]

So, let's ask ourselves—how do we act as the good Samaritan? How do we relieve the pain of the world? The pope says it best:

> We can start from below and, case by case, act at the most concrete and local levels, and then expand to the farthest reaches of our countries and our world, with the same care and concern that the Samaritan showed for each of the wounded man's injuries. Let us seek out others and embrace the world as it is, without fear of pain or a sense of inadequacy, because there we will discover all the goodness that God has planted in human hearts.[7]

In other words, in our broken world, we heal ourselves and we heal each other by imitating the Good Samaritan. We take care of each other. We tell the stories of the truth of our pain. We listen to stories of the truthful pain of others. And throughout our compassionate encounters, we bring recovery and reconciliation to our broken world and to our very own broken hearts.

FOR WHOM DO WE CARE?

For whom do we care? If you recall, this question was the title of the introductory chapter to this book. It is difficult to care about people we've never heard of, especially if they live far away and are not part of our daily lives. It is easier to care once we know them, or what is more likely, once we know *of* them. It is also easier to care about people experiencing disasters and atrocities, especially when highlighted in the news. But aside from these, we need to care about the ordinary and everyday people—the more than eight percent of the world's population that lives in poverty, the 22 percent of children under age five who suffer from malnutrition, the nine million people who die every year from hunger and hunger-related diseases, and the nearly one billion people who struggles with mental illness. These are the people who suffer, day by day, every day. They live close by and they live far away. These are the people for whom we must care.

---

6. Pope Francis, *Fratelli Tutti*, 74.
7. Pope Francis, *Fratelli Tutti*, 78.

And sometimes we fail to see the suffering of the people who walk right past our daily lives. The elderly neighbor. The poor little kids down the street. The homeless man in the back of the church. And the woman down the road with cancer. They are not extraordinary in any discernable way and their lives do not flash in the headlines, but they are people in need of compassionate encounters as much as those amidst disasters and atrocities, poverty and hunger, and physical and emotional pain. They are all like the needy stranger ignored by the Levites and the priests. They are all the people in need of compassionate encounters. *We* can be their good Samaritans.

MY PRAYER FOR YOU

We will sing in the morning and dance in the night,
> And if we shall meet, we will hold on tight.
> Then we'll paint away our tears and sweep to our delight.

Bibliography

Abulgasim, Fay, and Nariman El-Mofty. "Ethiopian Soldiers Said to Block Refugees From Entering Sudan." *Associated Press, The Minneapolis Star Tribune,* Dec 3, 2020. This story took place as the women fled an area of Ethiopia where a major assault was expected.

Alabed, Bana. *Dear World: A Syrian Girl's Story of War and Plea for Peace.* New York: Simon & Schuster, 2017.

Amiri, Farnoush. "House Votes to Honor Till, Mom." *Associated Press, The Minneapolis Star Tribune,* Dec 22, 2022.

American Psychological Association. "Education and Socioeconomic Status." Jul 2017. https://www.apa.org/pi/ses/resources/publications/education.

Arce, Julissa. "Trump's Anti-Immigrant Rhetoric Was Never About Legality — It Was About Our Brown Skin," *Time,* Aug 6, 2019. https://time.com/5645501/trump-anti-immigration-rhetoric-racism/.

The Associated Press. "Key Moments in Flint, Michigan's Lead-Tainted Water Crisis." *The Minneapolis Star Tribune,* Jan 12, 2021. https://apnews.com/article/us-news-health-michigan-rick-snyder-flint-7295d05da09d7d5b1184b0e349545897.

The Associated Press. "MN Regent Criticized for Asking if Campus is 'Too Diverse.'" *The Minneapolis Star Tribune,* Oct 18, 2022. https://apnews.com/article/education-minnesota-0852c0c4a9a5434e215e7b8fbc406d49. All student quotations are from this article.

Barry, Dan, and Sheera Frenkel. "'Be There. Will Be Wild!': Trump All but Circled the Date." *The New York Times,* Jan 6, 2021. https://www.nytimes.com/2021/01/06/us/politics/capitol-mob-trump-supporters.html.

Bickerton, James. "The 'Lady With the Big Teeth.'" *Newsweek,* Jan 19, 2023.

Biden, Joe, "Biden Takes First Tentative Steps to Address Global Vaccine Shortage." *The White House,* Mar 12, 2021. https://www.whitehouse.gov/briefing-room/speeches.

———. "Remarks by President Biden Announcing Response to Russian Actions in Ukraine." *The White House,* Feb 22, 2022. https://www.whitehouse.gov/briefing-room/speeches-remarks/2022/02/22/remarks-by-president-biden-announcing-response-to-russian-actions-in-ukraine/.

Boghani, Priyanka. "How the U.S. Has Reacted to China's Treatment of Uyghurs." *Frontline,* Nov 10, 2020. https://www.pbs.org/wgbh/frontline/article/us-reacted-china-treatment-uyghurs/.

Boms, Okechi, et al. "A Case For More (and More Ethical) COVID-19 Vaccine Trials In Africa." *Health Affairs*, Jan 20, 2021. https://www.healthaffairs.org/do/10.1377/forefront.20210112.870609

Bradshaw, Kelsey. *My San Antonio*, Aug 29, 2017, "President Trump in Corpus Christi: 'What a Crowd. What a Turnout.'" https://www.mysanantonio.com/news/local/article/President-Trump-visiting-Corpus-Christi-Austin-12132704.php#:~:text=During%20his%20visit%20to%20Texas%20in%20response%20to,crowd.%20What%20a%20turnout%2C%22%20according%20to%20media%20reports.

Brechtel, Evan. "Madison Cawthorn Got Called Out to His Face Over His 2020 Election Lies and He Just Dug Himself Deeper." *Second Nexus,* Oct 30, 2021. https://secondnexus.com/madison-cawthorn-confronted-election-lies.

Brown, Deneen L. "Tulsa Massacre Survivors Become Citizens of Ghana." *The Washington Post,* Mar 4, 2023. https://www.washingtonpost.com/history/2023/03/01/tulsa-race-massacre-citizenship-ghana/.

Brito, Ricardo, et al. "The Accused are United." *Reuters,* Dec 13, 2022. https://www.reuters.com/world/americas/bolsonaro-supporters-who-rioted-brasilia-will-face-punishment-says-future-2022-12-13/.

Brux, Jacqueline Murray. "COVID-19 Vulnerable Group Series," *River Falls News* (Note: the web site has been taken down, so please contact the author directly to receive the material.) https://riverfalls.news/NeighborhoodViews/VulnerableGroupsAmidstThe Coronavirus.

———. *Economic Issues and Policy,* 8th ed. New York: Wessex Learning, 2022. www.wessexlearning.com.

———. "Inequality and Racism as Structural Foundations of our Economy, Informed by Contempt and Perpetrated by Violence." Presentation: Southern Economic Association, Dec 2022.

———. "Yemen Vigil Handout." River Falls Social Justice, 2020 (unpublished).

Brux, Jacqueline Murray and Paige Miller. "Microenterprise Credit as Fundamental Reform: The Case of Kenya and Uganda." Presentation: Wisconsin Sociological Association, 2012.

Brux, Jacqueline Murray, et al. "Microcredit in Uganda: Fundamental Reform or Just Another Neo-Liberal Policy?" *African Journal of Economic Review,* Jul 2016.

Buckley, Chris. "Former White Supremacist: This is How to Tackle Hate and Bigotry." *CNN News,* Nov 12, 2020. https://www.cnn.com/2020/11/12/opinions/former-white-supremacist-how-to-tackle-hate-buckley/index.html.

———. "A Spring Thaw? Trump Now Has 'Very Good' Words for China's Leader." *The New York Times,* Apr 29, 2017. https://www.nytimes.com/2017/04/29/world/asia/trump-xi-jinping-china.html.

Bushard, Brian. "House Votes To Replace Bust Of Dred Scott Author." *Forbes,* Dec 15, 2022. https://www.forbes.com/sites/brianbushard/2022/12/15/house-votes-to-replace-bust-of-dred-scott-author-with-thurgood-marshall/?sh=33ea135e7cc5.

Camera, Lauren. "Biden: Trump Extremism 'Threatens the Very Foundation of Our Republic.'" *U.S. News,* Sep 1, 2022. https://www.usnews.com/news/politics/articles/2022-09-01/biden-trump-extremism-threatens-the-very-foundation-of-our-republic.

CBS News. "You Are The Elite." *CBS News,* Aug 4, 2018. https://www.cbsnews.com/video/trump-campaign-rally-2018-08-04/.

Chappell, Paul. "'He did not pray': Fallout Grows from Trump's Photo-Op at St. John's Church." *MPR News*, Jun 2, 2020. https://www.mprnews.org/story/2020/06/02/npr-he-did-not-pray-fallout-grows-from-trump-s-photo-op-at-st-john-s-church.

Chatelain, Ryan. "Tuberville, Greene Slammed for Racist Rhetoric at Trump Rallies." *Spectrum News*, Oct. 10, 2022. https://www.ny1.com/nyc/all-boroughs/politics/2022/10/10/tommy-tuberville—marjorie-taylor-greene-push-racist-rhetoric-at-trump-rallies.

Choiniere, Alyssa. "Central Park Five and Donald Trump." *Heavy*, Aug 21, 2020. https://heavy.com/entertainment/2020/08/central-park-five-donald-trump/.

Chute, Nate, et al. "Everything We Know So Far About the El Paso Shooting and How It Unfolded," *El Paso Times*, Aug 9, 2019. https://www.elpasotimes.com/in-depth/news/2019/08/09/el-paso-shooting-timeline-vigil-tragedy-trump-visit-beto/1932524001/.

Cillizza, Chris. "Donald Trump's Crowd Size Obsession Explains His Entire Presidency." *CNN News*, Jun 28, 2022. https://www.cnn.com/2022/06/28/politics/trump-crowd-size-obsession/index.html.

———. "Donald Trump's Emperor-Has-No-Clothes Moment on His Wealth is Here," *CNN News*, May 8, 2019. https://www.cnn.com/2019/05/08/politics/donald-trump-taxes-new-york-times/index.html.

Colbert, Harry, "Isolation And Feelings Of Being 'Unwanted' Confront Students Of Color At 'Too Diverse' University Of Minnesota Morris." MINNPOST, Oct 21, 2022. https://www.minnpost.com/opinion-pieces/2022/10/isolation-and-feelings-of-being-unwanted-confront-students-of-color-at-too-diverse-university-of-minnesota-morris/.

Concepcion, Summer. "Elaine Chao Issues Rare Rebuke." *NBC News*, Jan 26, 2023. https://www.nbcnews.com/politics/politics-news/elaine-chao-issues-rare-rebuke-trump-racist-attacks-rcna67605.

Corrigan, Kelly. *The PBS NewsHour*, Dec 9, 2020. This is regarding Attorney Bryan Stevenson.

Cramer, Philissa, and Ron Kampeas. "Kanye West's Vow to 'Go Death Con 3' on Jews and His Antisemitism Controversy, Explained." *Jewish Telegraphic Agency*, Oct 12, 2022. https://www.jta.org/2022/10/12/united-states/kanye-wests-vow-to-go-death-con-3-on-jews-and-his-antisemitism-controversy-explained.

D'Abrosca, Peter M., "Trump Blasts Jews Who Vote Democrat, Says They Show 'Great Disloyalty,'" *Loomered*, Aug 20, 2019. https://loomered.com/2019/08/20/trump-blasts-jews-who-vote-democrat-says-they-show-great-disloyalty/.

Duncan-Smith, Nicole. "'This Country Is Your Country': Tulsa Race Massacre Survivors Granted Ghanaian Citizenship and Property In the Motherland." *Atlanta Black Star*, Mar 8, 2023. https://atlantablackstar.com/2023/03/08/tulsa-race-massacre-survivors-are-granted-ghanaian-citizenship-and-property-in-the-motherland/.

Faiez, Rahim, and Siddiqullah Alizai. "In Afghanistan, Underground Schools Offer Hope for Girls." *Christian Science Monitor*, Aug 12, 2022. The teacher's name has been changed for her protection.

Fardah, Mentari Dwi Gayati. "Thousands of Workers Demonstrate Against Omnibus Law at DPR Building." *Antara Indonesian News Agency*, Jan 14, 2022. https://en.antaranews.com/news/209649/thousands-of-workers-demonstrate-against-omnibus-law-at-dpr-building.

Fink, Jenni. "Trump Says Jewish People 'Don't Love Israel Enough' Amid Complaint About Lack of Support." *Newsweek,* Jun 17, 2021. https://www.newsweek.com/trump-says-jewish-people-dont-love-israel-enough-amid-complaint-about-lack-support-1601576.

Flores, Reena. "Donald Trump's Feud with Bobby Jindal Escalates." *CBS News,* Sep 11, 2015. https://www.cbsnews.com/news/donald-trumps-feud-with-bobby-jindal-escalates/.

Francis, Pope. *Fratelli Tutti.* Encyclical letter. Rome: The Vatican, 2022. https://www.vatican.va/content/francesco/en/encyclicals/documents/papa-francesco_20201003_enciclica-fratelli-tutti.html.

Frontline-PBS. "China Undercover." Apr 7, 2020. www.pbs.org/wgbh/frontline/documentary/china-undercover. Frontline visited two Uighur sisters for this documentary.

Gabbatt, Adam. "Donald Trump's Tirade on Mexico's 'Drugs and Rapists' Outrages US Latinos." *The Guardian,* Jun 16, 2015. https://www.theguardian.com/us-news/2015/jun/16/donald-trump-mexico-presidential-speech-latino-hispanic.

———. "Outrage Over Alleged Nazi Homeschooling Group in Ohio." *The Guardian,* Feb 2, 2023. https://www.theguardian.com/us-news/2023/feb/01/nazi-homeschooling-group-ohio-condemned.

Gammage, Jeff, and Ximena Conde. "Bused Migrants Greeted in Philly With Open Arms." *The Philadelphia Inquirer,* Dec 4, 2022. https://www.inquirer.com/news/philadelphia/bus-immigrants-texas-philadelphia-asylum-greg-abbott-20221116.html.

Garamvolgyi, Flora. "Viktor Orbán Tells CPAC The Path to Power is to 'Have Your Own Media.'" *The Guardian,* May 20, 2022. https://www.bing.com/search?q=Garamvolgyi%2C+Flora.+%E2%80%9CViktor+Orb%C3%A1n+tells+CPAC+the+path+to+power+is+to+%E2%80%98have+your+own+media.%E2%80%99%E2%80%9D+The+Guardian&PC=IS42&PTAG=SYS1000003&FORM=ISCHR2.

Goertzen, Brenley. "There Was a Lot of Love: Trump Gushes About Jan. 6 Crowd in Newly Released Audio." *Salon,* Jul 22, 2021. https://www.salon.com/2021/07/22/there-was-a-lot-of-love-trump-gushes-about-jan-6-crowd-in-newly-released-audio/.

Go-Fund-Me. The Coaching Team College Fund for Marcus Hunter. Mar 2021. https://www.gofundme.com/f/wbhk8-marcuss-college-fund.

Gomez, Gregory Korte Alan. "Trump Ramps Up Rhetoric On Undocumented Immigrants: 'These Aren't People. These Are Animals.'" *USA Today,* May 16, 2018. https://www.usatoday.com/story/news/politics/2018/05/16/trump-immigrants-animals-mexico-democrats-sanctuary-cities/617252002/.

Hassan, Adeel. "Coronavirus Cases and Deaths Were Vastly Underestimated in U.S. Meatpacking Plants." *The New York Times,* Oct 28, 2021. https://www.nytimes.com/2021/10/28/world/meatpacking-workers-covid-cases-deaths.html.

Helderman, Rosalind S. "Trump Attacks American Jews on Truth Social Post." *The Washington Post,* Oct 16, 2022. https://www.washingtonpost.com/politics/2022/10/16/trump-jews-israel/.

Herman, Steve. "'Democracy Prevailed,' Biden Declares After Electoral College Vote." *VOA News,* Dec 14, 2020. https://www.voanews.com/a/usa_democracy-prevailed-biden-declares-after-electoral-college-vote/6199583.html.

Higgins, Andres. "Populist Leaders in Eastern Europe Run Into a Little Problem: Unpopularity." *The New York Times*, Oct 4, 2021. https://www.nytimes.com/2021/06/21/world/europe/eastern-europe-populist-leaders-unpopular.html.

Hodges, Betsy. "As Mayor of Minneapolis, 'I Saw How White Liberals Block Change.'" Opinion Exchange. *The Minneapolis Star Tribune,* Jul 10, 2020. https://www.startribune.com/betsy-hodges-as-mayor-of-minneapolis-i-saw-how-white-liberals-blockchange/571704812/#:~:text=In%20Minneapolis%2C%20the%20white%20liberals%20I%20represented%20as,applauded%20restoring%20funding%20for%20the%20rental%20assistance%20hotline.

Huff, Ian. "QAnon Beliefs Have Increased Since 2021 as Americans Are Less Likely to Reject Conspiracies." *Public Religion Research Institute*, Jun 24, 2022. https://www.prri.org/spotlight/qanon-beliefs-have-increased-since-2021-as-americans-are-less-likely-to-reject-conspiracies/.

Hunt, Elle. "Trump's Inauguration Crowd: Sean Spicer's Claims Versus The Evidence." *The Guardian,* Jan 22, 2017. https://www.theguardian.com/us-news/2017/jan/22/trump-inauguration-crowd-sean-spicers-claims-versus-the-evidence.

Hunter, Marcus. "I Live in a Cemetery Called North Minneapolis." Editorial. *The Minneapolis Star Tribune*, Mar 3, 2021. https://www.startribune.com/i-live-in-a-cemetery-called-north-minneapolis/600029485/.

Jones, Susan. "Biden Launches: 'We Are in the Battle for the Soul of This Nation.'" *CNS News,* Apr 25, 2019. https://cnsnews.com/news/article/susan-jones/biden-launches-we-are-battle-soul-nation.

Jordans, Frank. "Far Right Expected to Make Gains in German Regional Vote." *Associated Press,* Oct 26, 2019. https://apnews.com/article/immigration-international-news-germany-europe-9ab1d81f54894bac8fdedoc6180b2dao.

Judy, Alice, "The 84 Most Outrageous Donald Trump Quotes," *AnQuotes,* Jan 2, 2023. https://www.anquotes.com/donald-trump-quotes/.

Kamal, Zachary. "Mexican Asylum Seekers Set Their Sights North—On Canada." *Associated Press,* Nov 27, 2022. https://apnews.com/article/health-travel-mexico-immigration-covid-9534c9dc80e7ccbab605931a80d30613.

Kannuri, Nanda Kishore, and Sushrut Jadhav. "Cultivating Distress: Cotton, Caste and Farmer Suicides in India." *National Library of Health. National Institute of Health,* Nov 3, 2021.

Kessler, Glenn. "Trump Made 30,573 False Or Misleading Claims." *The Washington Post,* Jan 23, 2021. https://www.washingtonpost.com/politics/2021/01/24/trumps-false-or-misleading-claims-total-30573-over-four-years/.

Kossoff, Julian. "'Virtually the Entire Apparel Industry'—From Gap to H&M to Adidas—is Profiting From Forced Uighur Labor, Activists Say." *Business Insider,* Jun 23, 2020. https://www.businessinsider.com/uighur-forced-labor-global-brands-profited-activists-letter-2020-7.

Kruse, Michael. "The 199 Most Donald Trump Things Donald Trump Has Ever Said." *Politico,* Aug 14, 2015. https://www.politico.com/magazine/story/2015/08/the-absolute-trumpest-121328/.

Levine, Phillip B., and Melissa Kearney. "Early Childhood Education by MOOC: Lessons from Sesame Street." *National Bureau of Economic Research,* Sep 2016. https://www.nber.org/papers/w21229.

Low, Barbara J., and M. David Low. "Education and Education Policy as Social Determinants of Health." *The AMA Journal of Ethics, Policy Forum,* Nov 2006.

https://journalofethics.ama-assn.org/article/education-and-education-policy-social-determinants-health/2006–11.

Mahmood, Zahid, and Chris Stern. "Germany Arrests 25 Suspected Far-Right Extremists for Plotting to Overthrow Government." *CNN News,* Dec 7, 2022. fttps://www.cnn.com/2022/12/07/europe/germany-far-right-arrests-grm-intl/index.html.

Mannix, Andy. "Traffic Stops Criticized as Poor Policing." *The Minneapolis Star Tribune,* Apr 18, 2021.

Marchant, Bristow. "South Carolina County Settles Lawsuit over 'Debtor's Prison.'" *Minneapolis Star Tribune,* Dec 19, 2022.

Mastriano, Doug. "Praise Jesus!" and "Thank you Father God!!!" *Facebook,* May 29, 2022. www.facebook.com/SenatorDougMastriano.

Matthew, Zoie. "Crimes Against the Homeless Have Risen, and Advocates Are Searching for Answers." *Los Angeles Magazine,* Oct 15, 2019. https://zoiematthew.com/Homeless-violence.

McCarthy, Bill. "In Context: Donald Trump's 'Stand Back And Stand By' Debate Comments On White Supremacists." *Politifact,* Sep 30, 2020. https://www.politifact.com/article/2020/sep/30/context-donald-trumps-stand-back-and-stand-debate-/.

McCoy, Terrence. "Prejudice Against a Maid's Son." *The Washington Post,* Jun 28, 2020. https://www.washingtonpost.com/world/the_americas/brazil-racism-black-lives-matter-miguel-otavio-santana/2020/06/26/236a2944-b58b-11ea-a510–55bf26485c93_story.html.

McKenna, Amy. "Economic Freedom Fighters." *Encyclopaedia Britannica,* Mar 7, 2023. https://www.britannica.com/topic/Economic-Freedom-Fighters.

Miller, Andrew Mark. "Idaho Lieutenant Governor Holds Bible and Gun in Video Protesting Coronavirus Restrictions on 'God-Given Rights.'" *The Washington Examiner,* Oct 30, 2020. https://www.washingtonexaminer.com/news/idaho-lieutenant-governor-holds-bible-and-gun-in-video-protesting-coronavirus-restrictions-on-their-god-given-rights.

Mahamud, Faiza, and Jessie Van Berkel. "I Didn't Know We Were Hated." *Minneapolis Star Tribune,* Oct 13, 2019.

Mason, Margie, and Robin McDowell. "Palm Oil Labor Abuses Linked to World's Top Brands, Banks." *The Associated Press,* Sep 25, 2020. https://apnews.com/article/virus-outbreak-only-on-ap-indonesia-financial-markets-malaysia-7b634596270cc6aa7578a062a30423bb.

Mason, Margie, and Robin McDowell. "U.S. Blocks Malaysian Producer's Palm Oil." *The Associated Press,* Oct 1, 2020. https://www.ap.org/ap-in-the-news/2021/aps-mcdowell-mason-win-uw-madison-anthony-shadid-award.

Meyer, Jan. *Readers Write, Minneapolis Star Tribune,* Mar 5, 2023.

Micek, John. "Botched Executions Reached 'Astonishing High' in 2022, Report Finds." *The Pennsylvania Capital-Star,* Dec 20, 2022. https://missouriindependent.com/2022/12/20/botched-executions-reached-astonishing-high-in-2022-report-finds/.

Miller, Leila. "Brothers' Hope for Work Turned Tragic." *Los Angeles Times,* Jul 5, 2022. www.latimes.com.

Moses, Claire. "An Interview." *The New York Times.* Nov 27, 2022. Based on an interview with Natalie Kitroeff, the Time's bureau chief for Mexico, Central America, and the Caribbean. https://www.nytimes.com/by/claire-moses.

NPR MPR News, "Fact Check: Trump's Speech On Clinton, Annotated." Jun 22, 2016. https://www.npr.org/2016/06/22/483100251/fact-check-trumps-speech-on-clinton-annotated.

O'Connell, Gerard. "Pope Francis to Parents of L.G.B.T. Children: 'God Loves Your Children as They Are.'" *America: The Jesuit Review,* Sep 17, 2020. https://www.americamagazine.org/faith/2020/09/17/pope-francis-parents-lgbt-children-god-loves-your-children-they-are.

Otárola, Miguel. "Once Homeless, A Minneapolis Man Now Strives To Live In The Place He Helped Build.'" *The Minneapolis Star Tribune,* Apr 5, 2023. https://www.startribune.com/once-homeless-a-minneapolis-man-now-strives-to-live-in-the-place-he-helped-build/600000010/.

Parbarah, Azi, *the Washington Post,* Jan 26, 2023, "Does Coco Chow Have Anything To Do With Joe Biden's Classified Documents Being Sent And Stored In Chinatown?" https://www.washingtonpost.com/politics/2023/01/25/trump-elaine-chao-asian-americans-mcconnell/.

Parker, David L. (foreword by Senator Tom Harkin), *Before Their Time: The World of Child Labor.* New York: The Quantuck Lane Press, 2007.

Parrett, William, and Kathleen Budge. "How Does Poverty Influence Learning?" *Edutopia,* Jan 13, 2016. https://www.edutopia.org/blog/how-does-poverty-influence-learning-william-parrett-kathleen-budge.

Phillips, Tom. "Bolsonaro Targets the Catholic Church Over its 'Leftist Agenda' on the Amazon." *The Guardian,* Sep 23, 2019. https://www.theguardian.com/world/2019/sep/23/bolsonaro-targets-the-catholic-church-over-its-leftist-agenda-on-the-amazon.

Pierce, Charles P. "Georgia, Come and Collect Your Congressman. This is Embarrassing." *Esquire,* Dec 13, 2022. https://www.esquire.com/news-politics/politics/a42232258/rick-allen-mark-meadows/.

Pitofsky, Marina. "'Says a Whole Lot More About Him': Elaine Chao Speaks Out About Donald Trump's Racist Comments On Her." *USA Today,* Jan 27, 2023. https://news.yahoo.com/says-whole-lot-more-him-180500206.html.

Porterfield, Carlie, "Trump Says Jewish Americans Must 'Get Their Act Together' and Appreciate Him In Bizarre Truth Social Post," *Forbes,* Oct 16, 2022. https://www.forbes.com/sites/carlieporterfield/2022/10/16/trump-says-jewish-americans-must-get-their-act-together-and-appreciate-him-in-bizarre-truth-social-post/?sh=1fc1497253e8.

Rankin, Saran. "10 Accused of Smothering Black Mental Patient." *Associated Press, The Minneapolis Star Tribune,* Mar 17, 2023.

Raphelson, Samantha, "A Very Stable Genius': Trump Responds To Renewed Criticism Of His Mental State." *NPR MPR News,* Jan 6, 2018. https://www.npr.org/sections/thetwo-way/2018/01/06/576204103/a-very-stable-genius-trump-responds-to-renewed-criticism-of-his-mental-state#:~:text=%22Actually%2C%20throughout%20my%20life%2C%20my%20two%20greatest%20assets,genius...%20and%20a%20very%20stable%20genius%20at%20that%21%22.

Raskin, Jamie. "American Carnage is Donald Trump's True Legacy." *MSNBC News,* Jul 12, 2022. https://www.msnbc.com/msnbc/watch/raskin-refers-to-trump-s-inaugural-address-as-forecast-to-violence-of-jan-6-insurrection-143923269554.

Reals, Tucker, "Biden Pledges Up To $4 Billion To Help Get Poorer Countries Vaccinated Against COVID-19." *CBS News,* Feb 19, 2021. https://www.cbsnews.com/news/biden-covid-vaccine-covax-4-billion-pledge-poor-countries-coronavirus-equity/.

Reese, Thomas. "Pope Calls on World to Welcome Refugees and Immigrants." *National Catholic Reporter,* Sep 15, 2021

Reilly, Katie. "Read Hillary Clinton's 'Basket of Deplorables' Comment." *Time,* Sep 10, 2016. https://time.com/4486502/hillary-clinton-basket-of-deplorables-transcript/.

Reinl, James, and Zach Patnoe. "Slaughterhouses in Minnesota and Nebraska Use Child Labor for Sanitation." *The Daily Mail,* Dec 7, 2022. Cited in *Minneapolis Star Tribune.* https://www.bing.com/search?q=Comand+Zach+Patnoe%2C+Minneapolis+Star+Tribune%2C+11-23-2022.&PC=IS42&PTAG=SYS1000003&FORM=ISCHR2.

Ross, Madeleine. "God Loves Your Children." *The Daily Mail,* Feb 5, 2023. https://www.dailymail.co.uk/news/article-8750789/Pope-Francis-reassures-LGBT-people-God-loves-felt-church-did-not-accept-them.html.

Saavedra, Ryan. "DeSantis: 'Take A Stand Against The Left's Schemes' By Putting On 'The Full Armor Of God.'" *The Daily Wire,* Jul 24, 2022. https://www.dailywire.com/news/desantis-take-a-stand-against-the-lefts-schemes-by-putting-on-the-full-armor-of-god.

Sánchez, Diego Ibarra. "UN Renews Commitment to Yazidi Community." UNICEF, *Peace and Security, United Nations News, Global Perspective Human Stories,* Aug 3, 2022. https://www.unicef.org.

Sanon, Evans, and Dánica Coto. "UN: Children in Haiti Hit by Cholera as Malnutrition Rises." *United Nations,* Nov 23, 2022. https://apnews.com/article/health-caribbean-united-nations-port-au-prince-haiti-e5a94068b1c574f994092cba0ad38c53.

Santora, Marc, and Benjamin Novak. "Hungary's Migrant Abuse Is 'Matter of Urgency' European Agency Finds." *The New York Times,* May 21, 2019. https://www.nytimes.com/2019/05/21/world/europe/hungary-migrant-abuse-report.html.

Scoggins, Chip. "The Red Lake Nation Football Team Hasn't Won A Game In Years, But Its Coach Keeps His Kids Undefeated." *Minneapolis Star Tribune,* Dec 2, 2022. https://www.startribune.com/red-lake-nation-minnesota-football-team-coach-keeps-kids-undefeated-high-school/600226985/. All quotations in this section are from this source.

Seipel, Brooke. "Trump Again Claims No President Has Done More Than He Has In First Nine Months," *The Hill,* Oct 21, 2017. https://thehill.com/homenews/administration/356572-trump-again-claims-no-president-has-done-more-than-he-has-in-first/.

———. "Trump Blasts Liberal Elites: 'I'm Smarter Than They Are.'" *The Hill,* Mar 28, 2019. https://thehill.com/homenews/administration/436404-trump-blasts-liberal-elites-im-smarter-than-they-are/.

Shraffey, Ted, and Bobby Caina Calvan. "Central Park Entrance Honors Five Falsely Accused in 1989 Rape." *The Associated Press,* Dec 19, 2022. https://abcnews.go.com/US/wireStory/central-park-entry-gate-commemorates-exonerated-95565680.

Silverstone, Sylvia, "Trump Said He is 'Not Smart, But Genius . . . and a Very Stable Genius At That!' but Numbers Can't Seem to Prove His Claim." *MSN News,* Dec 22, 2022. https://www.msn.com/en-us/news/politics/trump-said-he-is-not-smart-but-genius-and-a-very-stable-genius-at-that-but-numbers-can-t-seem-to-prove-his-claim/ar-AA16dd1b.

Slawson, Nicola. "First Thing: Biden Warns US Democracy Imperiled by Trump Extremists." *The Guardian,* Sep 2, 2022. https://www.theguardian.com/us-news/2022/sep/02/first-thing-biden-warns-us-democracy-imperiled-by-trump-extremists.

Smith, David, et al. "Contagious Trump Removes Mask for Photos Upon Return From Hospital." *The Guardian,* Oct 7, 2020. https://www.pressreader.com/usa/the-guardian-usa/20201007/281663962469490.

Smith, Thomas R. "Dear Future." *International Times,* Jan 28, 2023. https://internationaltimes.it/dear-future/.

———. "Hand in Pocket, i.m. George Floyd." *Storm Island.* Northfield, MN: Red Dragonfly Press, May 30, 2020.

Snow, Hnin Ei Hlang (Director). *Midwives,* PBS Point of View AMA documentary film, Nov 21, 2022.

Sotomayor, Marianna, and Amy B. Want, "House Votes to Remove Bust of Justice Taney." *The Washington Post,* Dec 15, 2022. https://www.pressreader.com/usa/the-washington-post/20221215/281603834516888.

Specht, Paul. "Fact Check: Ad Attacks Beasley For Rulings in Sex Offense Cases." *WRAL News,* Jun 6, 2020. https://www.wral.com/fact-check-ad-attacks-beasley-for-rulings-in-sex-offense-cases/20318460/.

Spike, Justin. "Hungary to Host Conservative Conference For 2nd Time." *Associated Press, ABC News,* Jan 25, 2023. https://apnews.com/article/politics-united-states-government-hungary-viktor-orban-115b0b3356bb7c1fb5cd43c4f6260b1a.

Staff, Toi, "Health Ministry Official: Most People Will End Up Being Infected With COVID," *The Times of Israel,* Aug 9, 2021. https://www.timesofisrael.com/health-ministry-official-most-people-will-end-up-being-infected-with-covid/.

Stoops (ed.), Michael. "Vulnerable to Hate: A Survey of Hate Crimes and Violence Committed against Homeless People in 2013." *National Coalition for the Homeless,* 2013. http://www.nationalhomeless.org/wp-content/uploads/2014/06/Hate-Crimes-2013FINAL.pdfwww.nationalhomeless.org.

Stuart, Tessa. "Trump Is Happy to Inform Suburban Voters That He Is Still a Racist." *The Rolling Stone,* Jul 29, 2020. https://www.rollingstone.com/politics/politics-news/trump-suburban-voters-suburban-fair-housing-act-1032625/.

Tarlo, Shira. "Trump Wanted U.S. Forces Equipped With Bayonets to Stop Migrants at Border." *Salon,* Oct 4, 2019. https://www.salon.com/2019/10/04/trump-wanted-u-s-forces-equipped-with-bayonets-to-stop-migrants-at-border/.

Taylor, Darren. "Report Clearing Soldiers in South African Man's Death Sparks Anger." *VOS News,* May 29, 2022. https://apnews.com/article/health-travel-mexico-immigration-covid-9534c9dc80e7ccbab605931a80d30613.

Taylor, Miles, et al., "Trump Administration Insider: President Wanted to 'Maim' Migrants." *The Daily Beast, The New Abnormal Podcast,* Aug 25, 2020. https://www.thedailybeast.com/trump-administration-insider-president-wanted-to-maim-immigrants.

Thomsen, Jacquelin., "Trump: My supporters Should Be Called the 'Super Elite,'" *The Hill,* June 27, 2018. https://thehill.com/homenews/administration/394551-trump-my-supporters-should-be-called-the-super-elite/.

Timm, Jane C. "Trump Versus the Truth: The Most Outrageous Falsehoods of His Presidency." *NBC News,* Dec 31, 2020. https://www.nbcnews.com/politics/donald-trump/trump-versus-truth-most-outrageous-falsehoods-his-presidency-n1252580.

Tsongo, Esdras. "What is The Latest Conflict in the DR Congo About?" *Al Jazeera,* Jun 21, 2022. https://www.aljazeera.com/features/2022/6/21/explainer-what-is-the-latest-conflict-in-the-drc.

Trump, Donald. "The Full Text of Donald Trump's Inauguration Address." *The Guardian,* Jan 20, 2017. https://www.theguardian.com/world/2017/jan/20/donald-trump-inauguration-speech-full-text.

———. "Remarks by President Trump and President Al-Sisi of Egypt Before Bilateral Meeting." U.S. Embassy In Egypt, Apr 3, 2017. https://eg.usembassy.gov/remarks-president-trump-president-al-sisi-egypt-bilateral-meeting/.

———. "A Video Message from President-Elect Donald J. Trump." *The American Presidency Project,* Nov 21, 2016. https://www.presidency.ucsb.edu/documents/video-message-from-president-elect-donald-j-trump.

UNICEF. https://www.unicef.org/.

UNICEF. "UNICEF for Every Child." Feb 25, 2021. www.unicef.org/supply/covax.

———. "Building Bridges for Every Child: Reception, Care and Services to Support Unaccompanied Children in the United States." Feb 2021. https://www.unicef.org/reports/building-bridges-every-child.

Universe of Faith Inspirational Quotes, "Short Pope Francis' Quotes About Migration of Humans." Jun 22, 2016. https://universeoffaith.org/short-pope-francis-quotes-about-migration-of-humans/.

U.S. Catholic Sisters Against Human Trafficking. "International Day of Prayer Brings Awareness to Human Trafficking Worldwide." Jan 31, 2023. https://sistersagainsttrafficking.org/2023/02/international-day-of-prayer-brings-awareness-to-human-trafficking-worldwide/.

Useem, Jerry, "What Does Donald Trump Really Want?" *Fortune,* Apr 3, 2000. https://fortune.com/2000/04/03/what-does-donald-trump-really-want/.

U.S. Mission Egypt. "Remarks by President Trump and President Al-Sisi of the Arab Republic of Egypt Before Bilateral Meeting." *United Nations,* Sep 24, 2018. https://eg.usembassy.gov/remarks-by-president-trump-and-president-al-sisi-of-the-arab-republic-of-egypt-before-bilateral-meeting/.

Vazquez, Maegan, and Jim Acosta. "Jewish Leaders Outraged By Trump Saying Jews Disloyal If They Vote For Democrats." *CNN News,* Aug 21, 2019. https://www.cnn.com/2019/08/20/politics/donald-trump-jewish-americans-democrat-disloyalty/index.html.

Verbeek, David, and Andrew Davis. "Berlin Protest Against Virus Restrictions Ends in Clashes." *Bloomberg News,* Aug 30, 2020. https://www.bloomberg.com/news/articles/2020-08-29/tens-of-thousands-in-berlin-protest-against-virus-restrictions#xj4y7vzkg.

Vondracek, Cristopher. "Child Labor 'Not Really a Secret.'" *Minneapolis Star Tribune,* Nov 27, 2022. https://www.startribune.com/secret-not-a-secret-southwestern-minnesota-meatpacking-towns-react-to-child-labor-allegations/600230495/.

Wang, Amy B., and Marianna Sotomayor. "Booted From the Pedestal." *The Washington Post,* Dec 12, 2022. https://www.washingtonpost.com/people/marianna-sotomayor/.

The Washington Post. "'The Haitians all have Aids': White House Denies Donald Trump Made Offensive Remarks About Black Immigrants," *The Washington Post,* Dec 24, 2017. https://www.washingtonpost.com/news/global-opinions/wp/2017/12/28/no-president-trump-we-haitians-dont-all-have-aids/https://www.scmp.com/news/

world/united-states-canada/article/2125567/haitian-all-have-aids-white-house-denies-donald.

Winfield, Nicole, et al. "Your Tears are My Tears." *Business Mirror, The Associated Press,* Feb 2, 2023. https://businessmirror.com.ph/2023/02/02/pope-consoles-congolese-victims-of-violence-your-pain-is-my-pain/.

Winfield, Nicole, et al. "Pope Pleads for Respect for South Sudan's Women." *The Associated Press,* Feb 5, 2023. https://apnews.com/article/pope-francis-south-sudan-government-juba-e1ade89d06941ddod8d654d7e3e0978d.

Wong, Scott, and Peter Nicholas. "Cassidy Hutchinson's Jan. 6 Testimony Comes Under Increased Scrutiny." *NBC News,* Jun 29, 2022. https://www.nbcnews.com/politics/congress/cassidy-hutchinsons-jan-6-testimony-comes-increased-scrutiny-rcna35994.

Yan, Holly. "Donald Trump's 'Blood' Comment About Megyn Kelly Draws Outrage." *CNN News,* Aug 8, 2015. https://www.cnn.com/2015/08/08/politics/donald-trump-cnn-megyn-kelly-comment/index.html.

Yousafzai, Malala. *I am Malala.* New York: Little, Brown and Company, 2014.